PETER WISHART is the Member of Parliam
shire. He was first elected in 2001 and is th   member
for a Scottish constituency in the current House of Commons. He has held several responsibilities for the Scottish National Party at Westminster, including Chief Whip, Shadow Leader of the House, Constitution and Culture Spokesperson. For the past ten years he chaired the Scottish Affairs Select Committee. He is currently the Deputy Leader of the SNP at Westminster. Prior to going into politics Pete Wishart was a musician featuring in two of Scotland's iconic rock bands. Firstly Pete was a founding member of Big Country before joining Runrig, who have sold over 1.5 million albums worldwide. Pete recorded and performed with Runrig for 15 years. He was born and brought up in Dunfermline. Pete has been a columnist for a number of newspapers and runs his own blog which gives his own particular take on current political events. He is a keen diarist and this is his first book.

Inside the Indyref

PETE WISHART

Luath Press Limited
EDINBURGH
www.luath.co.uk

First published in 2024

ISBN: 978-1-80425-168-3

The author's right to be identified as author of this book
under the Copyright, Designs and Patents Act 1988
has been asserted.

The paper used in this book is recyclable. It is made from
low-chlorine pulps produced in a low-energy,
low-emission manner from renewable forests.

Printed and bound by
Robertson Printers, Forfar

Typeset in 11.5 point Sabon by
Main Point Books, Edinburgh

© Pete Wishart 2024

Images © Pete Wishart unless otherwise stated.

Thanks to the National Collective/Documenting Yes for kindly granting permission
to reproduce their photos.

This book is dedicated to all those independence activists who will not give up until our country is independent.

Preface

WHAT HAPPENS NOW?

This was the question we were all asking each other in the hours and days that followed the 2014 independence referendum when we had just been beaten 55–45% in the biggest exercise of participative democracy Scotland had ever experienced.

The result was decisive enough to be accepted by all parties but close enough to feel unresolved. How would Scotland respond to this result? Would that be it for a generation or would it be a springboard for a further, decisive contest? Was this a warm-up and taster for a future victory or the end of the independence dream? In the immediate days following the referendum no-one knew.

We were still haunted by memories of the 1979 referendum, a defeat that set back the campaign for a Scottish Parliament for a generation. This, however, didn't feel like that. Even in the early hours following this defeat something was happening. There was a defiance emerging, a determination to carry on the fight. The mood wasn't one of despondency, it was one of steely resolve.

The SNP and the Yes movement held several wash-up meetings in the days following the referendum and they were mobbed. I held one in Perth alongside MSP colleague John Swinney and there was barely enough room to get everybody in. The mood was not about giving up. It was about holding the winning No side's feet to the fire. It was about preparing for the next opportunity.

Then something else remarkable happened. Membership applications for the SNP went through the roof. The same happened to the pro-independence Greens. Opinion polls were starting to show decisive leads for the SNP and collapse in support for the unionist parties. A General Election was only a few months away and this presented the first opportunity to decisively show that the fight for independence was still alive. In that General Election the SNP won 56 of the available 59 seats on offer, recording almost 50% of the vote. If anyone believed that the cause of independence was over, they knew better now. The fallout from the referendum was to become ever-present in our political life and was set to reshape and redefine our politics and public life for the next decade.

Ten years on from the 2014 referendum and things are significantly different for the forces of independence. With no obvious route forward the Yes movement feels becalmed and uncertain. Many independence supporters have become alienated and the movement has fragmented into differing groups seeking solutions not on offer by the SNP. They are frustrated and disillusioned in what they see as a lack of progress in achieving their constitutional ambitions. Seventeen years of SNP Government has also had an impact. The SNP, like any government in power for such a long time, has not been immune to the swing of the political pendulum, burdened by familiarity and the expectation of constant delivery. This has had an inevitable impact on support and enthusiasm for independence. After a decade of SNP political dominance, we in the SNP have lost the 2024 UK General Election to a resurgent Labour Party in Scotland and are now in the fight of our lives to hold on to government in the Scottish Parliament.

The two key figures who were the main adversaries in the independence campaign are also no longer a feature of our political life. David Cameron, after successfully leading the union campaign as Prime Minister, was brought down after losing the referendum on EU membership a couple of years later. Brought back as Foreign Secretary by Rishi Sunak, he now faces the prospect of a life on the backbench in the House of Lords. Alex Salmond almost immediately stood down after the 2014 referendum and his attempt to return to frontline politics, after a lengthy and controversial court case, has failed to ignite much in the way of public interest. He now remains a diminished figure leading a party very much on the fringes of Scottish politics.

The excitement, energy and unity has gone and has been replaced by a fractured and restless movement that finds it increasingly difficult to replicate the drama and excitement of 2014.

But yet... Support for independence ten years after the referendum has shown levels of up to 50% in opinion polls, higher than the 45% secured in 2014. There are now more Scots who believe that independence is the most likely future for their country. Whilst independence may have gone down in the list of priorities of the Scottish people, it still remains an ever-present and key aspiration for so many Scots, a cause unwon and unresolved. The independence referendum has left a political legacy amongst Scots that will not be extinguished by the normal diet of everyday politics or cycle of election results.

This book covers the period leading up to the 2014 referendum. My diary entries capture the excitement and drama as well as the setbacks and disappointments of a political campaign the likes of which we have never seen before in a European democracy, and chronicle the debate in live time, taking the reader back to a year like no other in Scottish politics.

I've had this diary almost like a companion for the last ten years and I have thought long and hard about whether to have it published. Ten years on from the independence referendum and it now just feels like the right time to let it go. It is, of course, a personal account with my various takes on the unfolding events but I hope it resonates with everybody who was caught up in the drama of an exceptional year. I thought I would never get over the bitter taste of defeat in the morning of 19 September when it seemed like it was all over for those of us who believe that Scotland should be an independent country. The fact that the cause of independence endures and remains an aspiration for so many of our fellow Scots is a testament to all who threw absolutely everything into winning this contest.

Pete Wishart
August 2024

Introduction

I always wanted to show respect to the people of Scotland. I've made that referendum possible and made sure it's decisive, legal and fair, and I think that's right for the people of Scotland.
Prime Minister David Cameron in October 2012 following the signing of the Edinburgh Agreement setting the conditions for a referendum on Scottish independence.

DAVID CAMERON OF course had little choice. The Scottish National Party had just secured a majority in a proportionally elected Scottish Parliament in which such an outcome was supposed to be an impossibility.

From the moment that a majority was secured a referendum on Scottish independence became an inevitability. Downing Street initially showed just the right amount of disregard and defiance but almost immediately started to prepare for an independence referendum they knew they could not realistically resist.

Alex Salmond had won a majority in the Scottish Parliament on a clear manifesto commitment to deliver a referendum and all the conversations about devolved responsibilities and constitutional niceties were not going to change that hard reality one bit.

Setting themselves against a referendum would have taken constitutional tensions to an entirely new level and would have set in place a series of events beyond the UK Government's control. Alex Salmond had made it abundantly clear that there would be a referendum with or without the UK Government's consent, with all the chaos and confusion the latter would bring.

Above all, Cameron and the rest of the UK Government believed an independence referendum would be easily won. Such was Cameron's confidence that he conceded all the arrangements around the referendum, allowing the Scottish Government to set the date, the question and the franchise. The only thing the UK Government insisted on was that there would only be one question and that the referendum be held before the end of 2014.

The Edinburgh Agreement signalled the start of the campaign for Scottish independence and set in place one of the most keenly contested episodes in Scottish political history.

Just getting here was in itself remarkable and something few would have believed possible just a year previously. Up until two months before the 2011 Scottish Parliament election Labour held a double-digit lead over the SNP and were on course to become the largest party in Holyrood once again.

Labour had decisively won the 2010 election in Scotland and Scotland was the only part of the UK that recorded an increase in Labour's share of the vote. Then it all changed, and by April 2011 the SNP had pulled level and by the end of the month it was the SNP that held a double-digit lead over the Labour Party.

There were a number of factors behind Labour's spectacular collapse in the spring of 2011 but if anywhere can claim to be the birthplace of the independence referendum it is the unlikely setting of the Subway sandwich outlet in Glasgow's Central Station.

It was here the then Scottish Labour Leader, Iain Gray, sought refuge from a bunch of placard-waving protesters intent on stopping him campaigning against SNP cuts to an airport link. In extraordinary scenes those protesters pursued Iain Gray into the bowels of the property where Gray was awkwardly forced to confront the protesters in excruciating fashion in front of the TV cameras.

After eventually fleeing in a taxi he only went on to make the situation ten times worse by bizarrely comparing this experience to his time in Rwanda and 'the killing fields of Cambodia'. In one swoop Labour's 2011 election campaign was effectively dead. The SNP then went on to win a majority of seats in the election.

The SNP had secured one of the biggest electoral victories ever recorded in Scotland with a 44.5% vote share, the party's core mission of independence was supported by barely 30% of the Scottish public. The SNP had won the right to hold a referendum that was highly unlikely to be won.

To win we had to motivate, inspire and convince the Scottish people and campaign with a passion and conviction unseen in Scottish politics. Campaign teams were quickly assembled and the political battle commenced immediately but the first skirmishes were more of the phoney war variety. Until the spring of 2013 most of Scotland remained unfazed by the momentous decision that awaited them in just over a year's time. Opinion polls remained defiantly in favour of Scotland remaining in the union and the campaign to remain in the UK was cruising to what seemed like a certain victory.

Things were about to change and an unforgettable political drama was just about to be played out in one of the most unusual and exciting political battles ever experienced in a European democracy.

This account picks up the state of play from the end of June 2013 and it will take you through the day-to-day twists and turns in what was the most important political campaign this nation has ever participated in.

2013

The independence referendum campaign comes to life. Campaign teams are in place and battle has commenced but it looks like a mountain to climb for the forces of independence.

June 2013

Saturday 29 June

I've always kept diaries of my time in politics finding it cathartic to try and set out the developing political scene and to try to make sense of unfolding events. Writing it all down just helps clarify the issues for me and recording and reflecting the day gives me some sort of strange satisfaction and even a bit of solace and relief.

The independence referendum campaign feels just so different and seems so much bigger than anything that has happened before in my political life. I am therefore intending to write more extended entries and try and capture the prevailing mood and the developing agenda. All diaries start somewhere so today seems as good a day as any.

Sitting here at the end of June 2013 things are not looking all that encouraging for those of us who support the case for Scottish independence, and it's difficult to see how we're going to make progress in getting the majority we require. One thing we are going to have to do is get a lot more life into our so far moribund campaign.

The No campaign dominate the headlines. Their one task is to sew uncertainty and doubt about the viability of an independent Scotland and they have been singularly successful in pursuing this agenda. Their many questions about how an independent Scotland would operate has chimed with a sceptical Scottish public, unsure, or even hostile, to the whole independence proposition. In response we have been uncharacteristically timid and afraid to take chances. There is now a deeply embedded lethargy running throughout the whole Yes campaign.

Today I was at *The Scots Independent* newspaper's annual lunch at the Salutation Hotel in Perth. I was invited as a columnist and asked to say a few words to the more 'traditional' wing of the independence movement. Here the mood was more sanguine than hopeful amongst our most experienced and hardened of party veterans. Decades of bitter electoral defeat and disappointment has trained this particular cadre to be patient and to 'bide your time'. Their lesson is one that seems to have been assumed by the party as a whole. They show what a resilient but disciplined organisation we have become over these decades and how we are prepared to wait for that opportunity.

One thing that was missing was a sense of a campaign on its way to victory.

Just before retiring for the night a story was emerging that the No camp were claiming that Scotland would be hit by roaming charges in the event of independence. One of the now familiar and regular scare stories which dominate the referendum headlines. This runs contrary to everything that has been said in Europe about scrapping roaming charges throughout the EU. Doesn't matter though, the hit's been done, just as Scots are heading off to the beaches of Europe for their holidays. This just shows how far ahead of the game the Nos are and how they can get the hits they need, just at the time they need them.

Sunday 30 June

Last week the *Sunday Herald* ran a piece on Better Together and secured the gem that insiders refer to their job as 'Project Fear'. It took the party and Yes quite a while to recognise the significance and value of this admission and the opportunities it presented to us. This week all efforts have been on getting 'Project Fear' as an established phrase in the independence lexicon.

Today the Sunday papers are full of Project Fear related stories and there is a curious self-consciousness emerging from the No camp. This is a tag that they are not entirely comfortable with and are finding hard to run away from. Particularly liked the quote from veteran *Telegraph* columnist, Alan Cochrane, who said whoever came up with the phrase 'should be taken out and shot'. Quite what the Nos were thinking about letting out this leak would be anybody's guess, but it is singularly helpful to us.

July 2013

Monday 1 July

Today Alex made a speech about an independent Scotland belonging to five unions after independence. The EU, NATO, the Social Union, Currency and the Monarchy. The only union we will be severing is the political and economic union. Some commentators are again calling this 'indy lite' and that suits me just fine. Nearly every opinion poll prior to the Edinburgh Agreement found a majority for devo-max or indy lite, or whatever you want to call it. If we can appeal to this audience then we have an opportunity to get them into the Yes camp on a strong reassurance message. But we have to make a more direct pitch for that constituency than we're currently doing. Hopefully Alex's speech will start that conversation.

Tuesday 2 July

Alex's speech relatively well received and widely reported. Some unionists were a bit upset by the First Minister referring to them as a 'parcel of rogues'. I've been trying to wind them up even further by comparing these contemporary 'rogues' with their 18th century counterparts. Where the 18th century rogues traded in gold – the 21st centuries variety trade in fear and scare stories. Suggested that the 18th century 'rogues' made our contemporary lot look like bungling amateurs. They didn't like that one bit.

Surgeries round Highland Perthshire. I represent one of the most beautiful constituencies in the whole of the UK looking after a good part of the Central Highlands, East Perthshire and the city of Perth. Nowhere is nicer than the Perthshire Highlands. Reaching out from Dunkeld to beyond Rannoch Moor it takes in all the Tay river system, the Tay lochs, the Southern Cairngorms and iconic mountains such as Ben Lawers, Schiehallion and the Beinn A'Ghlo. It is stunning, and I love being here. I regularly hold surgeries in the area's largest towns and villages, Aberfeldy, Pitlochry and Dunkeld, and even if it's quiet it's good being seen out and about and available.

This was solid Tory country giving them amongst their biggest majorities in Scotland after the war, but we've dominated here for the past 20 years increasing our share of the vote at each subsequent election. Up here we're finding it difficult to secure support for independence, even amongst some of our most committed SNP voters, with a real distinction between support for the SNP and independence emerging. Quite hard to know what's behind it but there definitely seems to be an urban/rural and demographic edge to it. It's always presumed that the seats we hold will produce the biggest Yes vote. Not so sure that will actually be the case now. The Tories are in second place here and their voters are amongst the most resolute No supporters. They will depress the Yes vote in places like Perthshire but hopefully that will be offset from constituencies more receptive to our independence overtures.

Thursday 4 July

There's an important piece this morning from Jim Sillars. Jim has been a constant critic of our indy approach and because he is so far outside the SNP tent his observations come unburdened by concerns about press reaction. In a Scotsman column Jim acerbically notes: 'A comparison with the quality of the material produced by the Treasury and that produced by Salmond's office in recent weeks, shows a difference between a Premier League and a Third-Division outfit'.

He also poses a question that will in time come to haunt many of us SNP Parliamentarians. He asks: 'There is a question to ask of SNP backbenchers about the White Paper. What it says, or does not say, its substance or lack of it, will be one of the defining moments of the campaign. Whatever its content, SNP backbenchers will find themselves anchored to it. The question arises, therefore, if they are going to campaign for it, do they have a say in its content? Or will they see it only on the same day as the public, and thus, unlike the public who can be critical of it, be faced with the instruction from the Whips to give it unconditional support? Will they be excluded or included in its formulation? It's a fair question.'

It is indeed.

The White Paper is gaining such significance that its publication is being anticipated like some sort of constitutional tablet of stone. It is being prepared not by the party or the movement but by the civil service and they may not be sufficiently emotionally connected to our movement or to our cause. I also anticipate that Jim's 'premier league team' in the treasury, and elsewhere, are preparing to tear the white paper apart.

In other news it's reported that such is the turmoil in Yes that heads are set to roll. Seemingly all the resource in Yes is going on salaries and no-one is seeing a return. Nobody seems to know what we want from 'Yes'. Is it just cover for the SNP or is it now a real movement of its own? Movements of course need their own agendas, policies and hinterlands. What we have done is invent another independence campaign that is and isn't associated with the SNP and may or may not be in competition with us! Already the press are ever eager to play one against the other, and anything said by one that differs even in the slightest from the other is played out in full on the front covers.

The only reason the No camp haven't got properly stuck into all of this organisational shambles is that they are hamstrung by their own disastrous cross-party campaign, which if anything, is actually worse than ours.

Friday 5 July

This morning Westminster voted to hold an in/out European membership referendum putting it on a trajectory to completely withdraw from the EU. No SNP MPs were present at the vote and the whole debate only went to emphasise the different set of priorities between the UK and Scotland.

The Tory Government are pursuing this under pressure from the rise in the opinion polls of UKIP and tensions from their still unreconciled Euro-sceptic wing. The UK Government somehow believe that they can secure some sort of renegotiated EU membership package and put this in a referendum on EU membership. This is a particularly risky strategy and does nothing but embolden the many supporters of withdrawal within the Tory ranks. Such is the animosity towards the EU building up amongst Tory Euro-sceptics that even if the EU promised to redecorate the streets of London in gold there will still be a UK vote to leave the EU.

This is all very helpful as EU membership has become a massive indy issue with the various threats that we will be booted out with independence. If we can point to the Westminster Tories as the real threat to our EU membership we may just puncture this particular line.

This evening Andy Murray won his semi-final and will be appearing in his second Wimbledon final on Sunday. There's a huge story about his Scottishness and his sporting success that occasionally rears its head in the non-stop reporting of his incredible sporting journey. Such is the tone of the debate that it is going to be highly unlikely that any sporting stars will declare how they'll vote in the indyref. Most compete under the colours of the UK and I suspect that is where most of their allegiances will lie. Not so sure about Murray. The Saltire wristbands and the 'anyone but England' comments set him apart.

Sunday 7 July

Wimbledon tennis final and it was all going along as a wonderful triumph for Andy Murray with nothing other than the usual Scottish/British banter that accompanies Murray playing. A few unionists were trying to provoke a response on social media, but it was all low-level, pretty insignificant stuff. Then amidst the celebrations following his incredible victory Alex Salmond pulled out a massive Saltire right behind David Cameron's head. He just seemed to be standing there with his wife Moira waving it joyously. It was one of these 'am I believing what I'm seeing' moments and was quite hilarious in the stuffy, starch shirted environment of Wimbledon's Centre Court.

Unionists were completely blindsided and didn't know how to respond. They knew they had to attack him but were unsure on what basis. They couldn't attack our flag, or patriotism, so they went on the 'juvenile stunt' thing. Some did get carried away and a thread of anti-Scottishness started to appear on social media.

Monday 8 July

Today is all about that flag. Unionists still uneasy about their response and there is a sense of us backing down. We should be playing the indignant card. The sort of 'how dare they say where and when we fly our flag'. Of course we're not. I put something on these lines on social media and got an incredible response. Emailed Kevin Pringle and asked if we were going to follow up Alex's fantastic stunt? No, we weren't, Kevin tersely informed me, so the chance to take advantage of a key indy moment, gone.

Tuesday 9 July

Scottish Holyrood press pack on the House of Commons Terrace tonight. Don't get to see them much and they seemed genuinely pleased to see us. A curious and almost self-conscious bunch, they are the gatekeepers of the debate. We have a complicated relationship with this (on a whole) quite nice bunch of people. We of course spend too much time agonising over what they write about us. The thing is barely anybody reads their stuff anymore and it's an ever-diminishing audience for their hard worked copy.

All of the Scottish press is anti-independence and there are next to no journalists working in the Scottish mainstream press openly sympathetic to our cause. In the last few months a phalanx of independence-supporting websites and alternative media has emerged and they are increasingly becoming popular with independence supporters and those curious about our case. Though not in the same league as the mainstream press this development has certainly been helpful. We therefore do all we can to direct people to these sites and a lot of these sites have started to develop a powerful character of their own.

Another place where we dominate is on social media. The Yes campaign has made social media its own and it has helped spread our campaign themes and offer encouragement. The problem is that a lot of the conversation on social media is not always of the polished variety and the No campaign has been throwing everything to undermine our efforts by characterising a lot of the discourse as abuse and bullying. So far their efforts have not deterred the development of our online indy resource but how this plays out will be one of the key battle grounds in the message wars.

Wednesday 10 July

An adjournment debate in the name of Ian Davidson the chair of the silly Scottish Affairs Committee, on postal services in Scotland 'post 2014'. They of course wanted to have the debate titled postal services in a 'separate' Scotland but I got the use of the word separate banned from debate titles in the Commons. They had a similar debate with the 'separate' title timetabled a couple of months ago so I phoned the clerks up and asked what a separate Scotland was, and asked why a pejorative term was allowed in a Commons debate?

The clerks reasonably ruled that 'separate' should not have been allowed. The unionists were so angry and upset about this that they boycotted their own debate when they found they couldn't use their favourite pejorative term. Sensing a self-defeating stand-off the unionists skilfully negotiated a compromise where the words 'post 2014' would be used instead of 'separate'. Hilarious! So today was the first such 'post 2014/separate' debate. The timing couldn't be worse. Today was the day when Westminster announced that the Royal Mail was to be privatised.

Westminster group meeting tonight, probably the last before recess, so I used it to raise a number of issues. But first Angus Robertson went through, once again, his 500 business contact proposals. He wants us to get 500 businesses to meetings on independence in each constituency. Such is the support for independence amongst our business community we'd be lucky to get 15. Fair play to Angus, though. He's sticking to this. Instead of saying what I thought of the proposal I suggested that, why don't we get each parliamentarian to come up with three original suggestions in how we could shift the stagnant opinion polls on indy? I got the 'that's a good idea Pete' before it being completely mentally disposed of and forgotten about.

Later that evening we had the group and staff summer recess night out. Just as we were concluding our evening of pizza and chianti the news was coming through of Whitehall's plans to 'annex' Faslane, à la Cyprus, to secure the base for the rUK in the event of independence. This appeared in a *Guardian* article and was quite incredible in its almost imperial arrogance.

Thursday 11 July

Papers full of the annex story today and there is genuine rage that the UK would even consider annexing part of an independent Scotland. By 11am the plan was dumped by Number 10 and Cameron was distancing the Government from the *Guardian* story. It did though give an interesting insight into what is being considered in the dark recesses of Whitehall in the event of our success.

Sunday 14 July

At T in the Park today and it was typically brilliant and had a useful discussion with Festival Director Geoff Ellis. Watching some of the Scottish bands perform it struck me that we really need their support to ensure a majority of the under 30 vote. I remember how important cultural support for devolution was when nearly all of my contemporaries signed up for the cause of the Scottish Parliament. Bands and performers are such great ambassadors for causes and they build solid support and create valuable momentum. It also makes the cause cool amongst young people and independence must be seen as the cool choice.

The Yes group 'National Collective' is beginning to find its feet and starting to have an impact on artists and creatives but we still have a long way to go looking at what's going on here. So far we only have my (devolution) generation signed up for independence but we have to get Scottish bands like Frightened Rabbit, The View, and Twin Atlantic, who all played great sets yesterday. Predictably there was no-one there from Yes and you would have no idea that in just over a year we're having a referendum on independence.

Wednesday 17 July

Last PMQs of the term today and tried to get taken (ignored again). I've never had a question to Cameron since he was elected PM and have taken to standing to try to get in. Miliband was truly awful and was trounced by a confident Cameron bolstered by opinion polls and Labour's union woes.

MP4 rehearsal tonight. I put together our parliamentary rock band with Ian Cawsey about ten years ago and we've gone on to be a Parliamentary institution. Totally cross-party and coming from constituencies across the UK, we are the only Parliamentary rock band anywhere in the world. We've played all the party conferences and even recorded an album with top record producer Robin Millar. It's great fun and over the years we have all become good friends and have risen to the giddying heights of just about competent. We're playing the Musicians' Union next week, so a tougher audience than usual but confident we will be treated kindly.

Friday 26 July

With our External Affairs Minister Humza Yousaf all day in a variety of events to develop links and secure support from Perthshire's ethnic minorities. Humza is a capable, talented and very likeable young man. At the age of 28 he is our youngest Minister and has featured twice for us on *Question Time*. Just to curse his prospects it has even been said that he is a possible future First Minister. Humza worked for us at Westminster before swapping Westminster for Holyrood to work for the late Bashir Ahmad, whose Holyrood list seat he inherited when Bashir died. He's also great fun to be with and I have been working with him in developing some of the materials in the citizenship and immigration part of the White Paper.

Support shouldn't be too hard to secure from Perth's South Asian community. I was the first Perthshire Parliamentarian to visit the Perth Mosque and have retained very good relations having helped countless Perthshire Asians resolve their many immigration difficulties over the years. We visited the mosque and met the local committee where it became apparent that, whilst there may be questions, their support was more or less assured.

Later Humza and I had an opportunity to talk over the immigration and citizenship parts of the White Paper. My view is that we have to do as little as possible to the rest of the UK so that they can't threaten us with border posts and restricted travel. We are going to stick to the points-based system and continue with the common travel area throughout the UK, whilst doing what we can round the edges to suggest some sort of different approach.

Last event was a Scots for Independence meeting in the Fair Maid's House in the city. It was predictably quiet for 3pm on a Friday afternoon and Roseanna Cunningham's staff, who organised it, invited a stellar cast. We had the top human rights lawyer, Aamer Anwar and Euro candidate Tasmina Ahmed-Sheikh as well as Humza, Roseanna and me. For the 50 or so members of the public who attended they heard from two Government Ministers, an MP, and three top human rights lawyers.

Sunday 28 July

First opinion poll on independence for months today and it is a bit of a mixed bag. Coming from Panelbase it shows a rise of 1% in our support taking us to 37% but it also shows a rise of 2% for the

Nos taking them to 46%. This is actually encouraging as I thought we would be struggling to get over 30% just now. Importantly, what it shows is that we only need a swing of 5% to take the lead. The party is obviously very happy with this and everyone sharing the poll on social media. Another factor that has been picked up by the media is on the 'likely to vote' category and that strongly favours us. Think the No camp will be just a little bit exercised and concerned this morning.

It's been difficult getting people out to canvass (or any activity) to support the Yes campaign and the regular Thursday night canvassing is usually just me and one or two others. This is curious as we (the party) should be totally focussed on winning the referendum and one would have expected a huge and overwhelming commitment. Many reasons are given for the lack of activity ranging from anxiety about the questions that may be asked on the doorstep to the belief that there is still a lot of time left till the referendum. If we're going to win this we will have to get in front of people and seek to persuade them.

August 2013

Saturday 10 August

It's the kilt run in Perth this morning. Perth is attempting to break the world record for runners in kilts and the whole city is quite excited about it. I went to bed early last night in preparation and of course didn't sleep a wink. Done a bit of training but this will now count for nothing given my lack of sleep state. Worse than that I have to get back and changed and up to the Black Isle for Runrig's 40th Birthday Show. Sure I'll get through the day but just now I'm not entirely sure how.

Did the kilt run in an impressive 31 minutes and was very pleased with it. We broke the 'official' record with 1,300 or so runners but Perth Canada still has the 'unofficial' record of 1,800. Unfortunately for Perth Canada they didn't properly register it with the Guinness World Records. So way to go Perth Scotland.

The Runrig gig was great and I was asked up on stage with my former colleague, singer Donnie Munro. Donnie's a curious figure who stood twice (unsuccessfully) as a Labour Parliamentary candidate. Donnie would almost certainly have been Scotland's first culture secretary if he had managed to get those last few hundred votes in the first Scottish Parliament election in his home constituency in Skye. A very impressive man with a huge intellectual hinterland and bucketloads of charisma, Donnie at the height of our success was just about the most recognised man in Scotland.

Where all the rest of the Runrig guys made the journey from Labour to the SNP through the '80s and '90s Donnie remained resolutely Labour mainly down to his friend and political mentor the former Labour Minister, Brian Wilson. The Donnie I met tonight, though, seemed genuinely conflicted about the independence referendum. He had dinner in Skye with the First Minister the previous week and Alex had obviously made his usual impressive impact. Would be great if Donnie completed this journey and joined the rest of the 'Runrig' family on the Yes side.

No such issue with the other performers present. Julie Fowlis, the singer in the animated film Brave, is a huge supporter and told me she is meeting Nicola Sturgeon this week. That also goes for top fiddler Duncan Chisholm and rising Gaelic stars, Mànran. Was a great night and will always be grateful to the Runrig guys for their support, encouragement and for just being the incredible talents that they are.

Tuesday 13 August

Woke up to the news that an American 'polling expert' was predicting that Yes have virtually 'no chance' of winning the referendum. The man in question was Nate Silver, and his credentials seem to be based on the fact that he predicted the correct result for each state in the last American election. This proved to be so newsworthy that the Scotsman put it on its front page. Almost like a red rag Yes types immediately started burrowing around Mr Silver, and lo and behold, they found that this (always right) American called the last UK election wrong. Almost unembarrassed by this revelation the story even continued to get prominence for the rest of the day.

In the afternoon I was on a panel for the British Youth Council with Willie Rennie, Lab MSP Drew Smith, Tory councillor David Miekle and the Yes campaign's Gail Lythgoe. The audience were a mixed bunch of articulate and politically turned-on young people and the debate was mainly consensual. Young people's voting intentions in the indyref are still pretty much a mystery but there is good evidence that we are doing badly with the under 20s. We thought that young people would be the most eager Yes supporters and their reticence has surprised us. Don't know how we'll turn this round but know that more work certainly needs to be done.

Wednesday 14 August

The Yes campaign was arguing its case with 'all the passion of a robot'. This was the withering assessment of former SNP leader, Gordon Wilson, in this morning's papers. He went on to say that 'there is an absence of vision, passion and emotion. National freedom does not exist in a sterile environment'. Typically blunt, it is a view that chimes with a large constituency in the party who feel that we are not pushing the Yes cause with the necessary dynamism.

Gordon Wilson is a prickly figure with a range of views and opinions that sits uncomfortably with the general message of the party and he inevitably went on to spoil this with a silly attack on the 'cancer' of the south of England, and calling for further referendums on the EU and the monarchy. The result is that his criticism of the tone of the campaign will be lost in the more bizarre comments. Gordon has also emerged as one of the main opponents of equal marriage and his credibility amongst most people in the party has therefore been diminished if not lost completely. It would also have to be said that under his disastrous leadership our current campaign would look positively exciting compared to his thoroughly dismal leadership style. Probably, just as well then, he will never be seen as a figure who those unhappy with the way the referendum effort are going to congregate around.

Almost like a gift to the Yes side today is the day that Scotland plays England at Wembley. Twenty-thousand passionate Scots have descended on London and the rest of the nation is wrapped up in that warm soft Scottish patriotism that accompanies Scotland football games.

So what has Yes and the SNP done to try and motivate this Scottish enthusiasm into support for Yes? Absolutely nothing. Almost unbelievably we have backed off saying anything about the game other than the usual banal 'good luck Scotland' messages. There is obviously a bit of work to do to pitch for the 'Scotland support' constituency without being gratuitous and blatantly obvious but no-one is even thinking about starting this crucial work, and probably no-one will.

England eventually won a fantastic game 3–2 where Scotland led twice. Great behaviour from the Tartan Army and you would hardly have thought that we were a year out from an epoch defining referendum.

Thursday 15 August

There's been a meeting with the Scottish Government and NATO. The unionist-supporting press report this as a dressing down for Yes, a sort of 'you don't get into our club unless you accept our nukes' telling off. Then there is the Yes side reporting it as a meeting of minds.

It's hard to imagine the North Atlantic Treaty Organisation not accepting Scotland as a member as you can't get more North Atlantic than Scotland and we couldn't be more strategically important at the point where the North Sea meets the Atlantic at the bottom of the Iceland Pass. But I'm also pretty sure that the UK Government have made their position clear to their allies and they would expect NATO to make life as difficult as possible for us.

The SNP of course made NATO membership an iconic issue. Uniquely, of all the policy 'refinements' of the past year NATO was properly debated at our last conference. In what was a high-quality debate the party narrowly supported a motion supporting NATO membership dependent on Scotland being a non-nuclear state. It lost us two MSPs but it was the right thing to do. Going into the referendum anti-NATO would be almost indy suicide. However, being non-nuclear is an absolute red line and even those like me who are prepared to set the bar as high as possible to get a Yes vote could never accept a compromise in our non-nuclear commitment.

Sunday 18 to Saturday 24, 2013: in Catalonia

Two days in Barcelona, two in Girona and two on the coast in Calella. Fantastic time learning more about the Catalan independence movement. Spent the week speaking to commentators, politicians, academics and campaigners. There is absolutely no doubt whatsoever that independence is the settled will of the Catalan people and there is a clear majority in favour. I'm here in advance of the 'Catalan Way' the human chain which will run the length of the country. Four-hundred-thousand people will link arms in the cause of Catalan independence and if anything it will be oversubscribed. This is to be held on the Catalan national day and follows the 1.5 million that marched in Barcelona the previous year.

Madrid is still refusing to engage in the debate about Catalan independence and continue to say no to any referendum leading to what is becoming a pretty tense political stand-off. The pro-independence parties are therefore considering what options they have. One thing being considered is dissolving the Catalan Parliament and causing elections where all the pro-independence parties stand on a manifesto exclusively on independence. This, they believe will give them a mandate for independence if a referendum continues to be forbidden. It is also a very risky strategy and everyone I spoke to was unsure about the way forward and how exactly the independence process will be advanced.

In my trip I also addressed a large open-air rally in Calella, sponsored by the independence-supporting left-wing party Esquerra. This would be something that would not be viewed favourably back home. Angus Robertson has made it very clear that we should not be getting involved with the independence movement here with the fear that Spain would start to get aggressive about our European entry ambitions. That is a view that I see as pretty pointless as Spain will always make life difficult for us regardless of what we do as long as the cause of Catalan independence remains on the agenda. The Catalans do want to make more of a common cause with us and we should be supporting them as comrades seeking the same outcome. The very least we could be doing is highlighting the shameful behaviour of the Spanish Government in refusing the Catalan people their referendum. Still keeping an eye on the Scottish indy news while over here and a couple of very big stories emerged this week and even being away I was still at the end of journalists' phones.

First up was *The Guardian*'s Severin Carrell with a story about comments from the Director General of the Commonwealth who suggested in an interview that an independent Scotland might not get into the Commonwealth, as the approval of all members would be required. The story is similar, if not identical, to entry issues of other multilateral institutions like the EU, NATO, etc.

The Commonwealth is probably just about the worst possible example to raise on the 'no entry' scaremongering agenda as membership of the Commonwealth is almost exclusively based on securing independence from Westminster. This didn't stop the press from having a field day.

Gave Sev some comment and the next day my phone was red hot from other journalists wanting further comment and I couldn't believe that here I was in Barcelona talking about Commonwealth membership!

The really big story of the week though is that Yes Scotland's email system seems to have been hacked. Yes became suspicious when they were approached about a story that they had made a payment to an academic to write a favourable article which appeared in *The Herald*. Yes knew immediately that this could only have come from unauthorised penetration of its systems. The Nos and most of the press were little interested in the hacking and instead focussed on the 'payment' story as an example that we cannot be trusted and are even prepared to pay 'bungs' to plant stories. The fact that we had our systems hacked was supremely unimportant to them. Just wait till it happens to the Nos.

Sunday 25 August

The UK Government have decided to hold the UK Armed Forces Day in Scotland, in Stirling in fact, on the same week that the 700th Battle of Bannockburn is being commemorated. The UK Government aren't even pretending that this is anything other than a huge unionist stunt designed to show the strength and unity of the UK's armed forces and take the edge off the Scottish patriotism that will inevitably emerge from something as iconic as Bannockburn. Very impressed with Veterans Minister, Keith Brown's, dignified response welcoming the event and saying he didn't care about the UK Government's motives.

The *Sunday Express* covers a hilarious story saying that almost half a million people may leave Scotland if we become independent. They even reported that a large part of this group may be Tory voters. We all had great fun suggesting that the M74 might be crammed full of Tory 4x4s fleeing the 'Salmond dawn'.

Monday 26 August.

Syria really hotting up with all sorts of threats of military action following the chemical weapons attack. Cameron would really like to get involved and he has repeatedly talked about arming the rebels. Today it's gone further with suggestions of military strikes. We put out a press release to say that Parliament must be recalled before any military action is considered, joining many other Parliamentarians. Military involvement would be a disaster for the UK making Iraq seem like a walk in the park and this could soon be an issue that will put all others (including the referendum) aside.

Tuesday 27 August

Parliament will actually now be recalled on Thursday with a debate (and a vote) on Syria and possible military action. Given there is a vote it must mean that Cameron has done a deal with all the other front benches as he would not risk a substantive no vote to any escalation. It seems very unlikely that we will support any unauthorised military intervention and already the press are getting in touch about what we are likely to do. The last time I was recalled to Parliament in such circumstances was to debate Labour's 'dodgy dossier' in 2002. This time round the evidence for action could be just as flimsy.

Wednesday 28 August

Incredible developments on Syria. Just when it looked like Labour had signed up to the Tories intention to embark on military action they've only gone and pulled the rug. Labour are now talking about voting against the Government and there is also talk of putting in their own motion. We have put out a fairly bland press release and Angus Robertson is in London negotiating with the Labour Party and others about what we should do. Just hope Angus doesn't sell us too short to Labour. Later we see the Government's motion and it talks about the 'possibility' of military action and it is much watered down. There is also speculation about a further debate and vote next week depending on what the UN inspectors find.

Thursday 29 August

Back at Westminster for the Syria debate and the atmosphere is incredible. First stop is a meeting of the SNP group to discuss what we're doing and hear an update from Angus Robertson. We're seemingly a co-sponsor of the cross-party motion requiring UN resolutions, international law and evidence. Where I'm a bit uncomfortable about signing up with Labour I accept Angus Robertson's reasons of being seen to be part of the Parliamentary and public consensus.

The debate is quieter than I expected with both Cameron and Miliband subdued. Cameron clearly irritated, put his case with all the conviction he could muster. Miliband started with this adopted statesman tone before resorting to his usual stumbling delivery after some difficult interventions. Expected more fireworks following the obvious acrimony between the two of them in the lead-up to the debate. The debate was closed by an absolutely dreadful speech from Nick Clegg that could have done nothing other than encourage the

Liberal backbench to consider voting against the Government.

No-one could have prepared us for what was to happen next. After our cross-party motion was heavily defeated no-one was actually paying all that much attention to the Government's decisive resolution. Then all sort of commotion started in the lobbies. I was in conversation with some Labour whips just outside the Aye lobby when I noticed a real agitation on the Government whips' faces. This turned to real alarm when they started to observe the sheer number of Tories going through the No lobby.

This agitation descended into blind panic when news of a Government defeat started to emerge. Then the result. A Government defeat by 13 votes. Totally unexpected and out of nowhere. In the chamber Cameron's face was ashen and Michael Gove resorted to shouting 'Appalling! Appalling!' to everyone leaving the chamber like some sort of contorted pantomime dame. Cameron had to get to his feet and acknowledge what had happened and, credit to him, he immediately said that parliament had spoken and its view would be respected.

Absolutely jubilated, we went home still a bit shell shocked about what had just happened.

Friday 30 August

Everybody digesting what this Government defeat means. It is accepted that the UK will play no part in any action and that there will be no immediate second vote. Blame is being apportioned and the UK parties are hitting out viciously at each other. It seems that Cameron had offered Miliband practically everything he wanted to secure cross-party consensus on the motion and had conceded to nearly all his requests. Feeling he had a deal Cameron proceeded only for Ed to pull the rug out from under him on the final outcome.

There also seems a major fault at the heart of the Government whips' office. About 80 Tory MPs didn't turn up for the vote and there were even two Government Ministers who were on the Parliamentary estate but did not make it to the division lobbies for the decisive vote. My initial thought is that this defeat is more cock-up than Labour tactical organisation.

September 2013

Sunday 1 September

New poll out and it's a disaster.

For the first time in months we are below 30% coming in at a paltry 29% with 59% for No. There are absolutely no positives to be taken from this and the party and Yes thankfully remain quiet and refrain from trying to spin anything out of it. Can't say that I didn't see this coming, just surprised it's taken so long to get here. Regardless of how bad this is I still don't believe it will kick start any sort of reassessment and change of emphasis or tone.

The only piece of good news is that it's reported that Kevin Pringle is to be drafted into the Yes campaign. Kevin has a political instinct almost unparalleled in Scottish politics and everyone defers to him on tricky issues. He is also a thoroughly nice guy who I've worked with for over 12 years. Unassuming, bordering on shyness, he can also come across as a commanding and forceful presence when roused. Just hope he can make a difference.

What we now need are big motivational speeches from Alex and Nicola, people with the ability to inspire drafted in and dispatched. Less responding to the Nos' agenda and more of an emphasis on what Scotland could do with its independence.

We need to inspire and inject a bit of passion. More than anything we need to believe in our case.

Tuesday 3 September

Woke up to George Osborne giving a disastrous interview on Good Morning Scotland. He's in Aberdeen launching the UK Government's fifth anti-independence paper and he's telling the oil industry why they need his Tory Westminster Government to run their affairs. Norway has an oil fund of £470 billion and rising and Scotland has food banks and years of austerity. Yet Osborne persists that Scotland needs his disastrous stewardship. It is an awful interview and there will be more than a few Labour members listening to this wondering how they managed to get into a position of being on the same side as a right-wing Tory Chancellor.

In the Commons it's the register of lobbying, non-party campaigning and trade union bill, the so-called 'gagging' bill. This is probably the worst drafted bill that I have seen in my 12 years as an MP and it has infuriated charities and third-party organisations. They have all been caught up in the new regulations which will be imposed on them in the year up to the next general election. What the bill does is limit the role they can play in helping impact political change and put forward their agenda to politicians. My mail bag has been full of angry constituents concerned about their favourite charity and the 'gagging' of their role in democratic debate. In the debate this bill was torn apart by members of all parties. It still passed though with a large majority. Once again, the vast majority of Scottish members of Parliament voted against the bill. It will be imposed on Scotland anyway.

Wednesday 4 September

Off to Poland today to the Economic Forum at Krynica where I'm on a panel to speak about independence movements in Europe. Just started to realise what a big deal this is. The Economic Forum is described as the 'Davos of the East' and it is huge. Arrive very late after a three hour flight from London and a further two hour drive to Southern Silesia but it looks quite an event.

Thursday 5 September

Awake to the beautiful sight of the southern Silesian mountains and my first thought is I better write something for today's appearance. The conference village is massive with thousands of delegates and loads of panels with big names. I'm on a panel with a Catalan, a

Serbian, a German and, for some reason, a Democratic Unionist politician. I describe how our independence movement is distinctly different from all the other independence movements of the post-Soviet era saying that Scottish independence has nothing whatsoever to do with ethnicity or culture.

In my contribution I say that we've never been oppressed by anybody and our movement has nothing to do with historic grievance or animosity. The cause of Scottish independence is entirely civic and peaceful and no-one has even had a bloodied nose from our cause. We want our independence despite the fact that we are culturally secure because we believe we can do things better if we run things ourselves and make our own particular international contribution. I patiently explain this today, and sense that there is enormous goodwill for our cause. I think that there is a real desire to see us win because it could be the way forward for new nations and our process. Fantastic day here in Poland and made many new friends and allies.

Wednesday 11 September

Scottish Questions gets its monthly outing this morning and it is as usual a thoroughly depressing affair. The key dynamic of Scottish questions is Scottish Labour MPs ask questions berating independence only for these coalition Ministers to agree with them and then berate independence even further. It's actually quite amusing and it gets even better when English back bench Tories get stuck in. In Parliament there are 650 members and practically all loathe the very idea of independence. There are the six of us and our three Plaid Cymru colleagues taking on the vast ranks of Labour, Liberal and the Tory-led Government. With those forces ranged against us we don't do too badly.

After Questions I raise a point of order. I had carefully planned this anticipating a positive response from the Speaker. Yesterday I saw that Labour's Anas Sarwar had a question which referred to a 'separate' Scotland. After my success at having 'separate' banned from debate titles I thought I'd chance my arm and see if it could have it proscribed in questions too. The first clerk I spoke to immediately knew there was an issue and I was passed up to the chief clerk who told me that it should not have been allowed on the order paper as it was 'argumentative'. He said he wouldn't take it off in advance of questions today because, in his view, it would cause even more of a fuss after being approved by our Table Office. I said that I would then make a point of order to ensure it wouldn't happen again. He accepted this and said that was in my right. I then phoned the Speaker's office and told them of my intentions.

After questions I therefore asked the Speaker if he knew what a 'separate' Scotland was and asked him to agree that it was a pejorative term used by the opponents of independence. I mentioned that the clerks said it shouldn't have been on the order paper today and would he assure me it wouldn't feature in questions again?

In response he did more than that. He said the term that should be used is in fact – independence. Brilliant! Labour were furious. I hadn't consulted them and I made sure not to mention Sarwar so there was no need for prior notification. They tried to heckle and shout me down but it was done. 'Separate' is banned from questions and I felt great securing this totally inconsequential and singularly unimportant little victory. But when you see the odds stacked against us in the House of Commons it's these little victories that taste fantastic.

Sunday 15 September

The big debate today is about who is debating who. There are several articles kicking around this morning on who should be involved in the main debates and it is really interesting how this is being lined up. The unionists are doing all they can to keep Cameron out of any debate with the First Minister to avoid any sort of Scotland verses the UK inference. We in the meantime are doing all we can to ensure that this is exactly what happens. Alistair Darling is staking his place in the main debates claiming his place as head honcho of 'Better Together' Where he might lead Better Together, he is little more than a backbench MP, and his equivalent is Dennis Canavan as the leader of Yes. I suggested that the debates should be Cameron vs Salmond,

Canavan vs Darling and Blair Jenkins vs Blair McDougall adding it couldn't be fairer than that. Unionists predictably disagreed.

Tuesday 17 September

The Liberals are in Glasgow for their national conference and they seem to be tripping over each other to comment on the indyref. This morning it's reports that Michael Moore is comparing the SNP to UKIP. This is an old and tired trope that does the rounds when they can't think of anything else to say about us. This rest of 'Better Together' don't seem to want to touch this with a barge pole and seem to be leaving it to the Libs. In Scotland the Liberals are a rejected party reduced to a rump who couldn't win a mainland seat at the last Scottish election. They now also seem to be determined to seal their reputation as outsiders in the indyref debate with stuff like this. Good luck to them.

Another big Yes public meeting tonight in Perth. About 150 people turned up at a packed AK Bell theatre. Very good meeting with Blair Jenkins, Carolyn Leckie and John Swinney. The one thing that the indyref has done is revitalise the idea of the public meeting and people are turning out in their droves to events such as this. This is the third one we've held in my constituency which has secured more than 150 people and this is remarkable. The one thing that the indyref is doing is reconnecting people with politics and the interest the indyref is generating can only be good for our democracy.

Thursday 19 September

The Institute of Fiscal Studies has today concluded that we could be faced with a £5.9 billion black hole in the event of independence. This is based on a very pessimistic view of the income from North Sea Oil (the almost nonsensical Office of Budgetary Responsibility figures) and 'planned' UK spending cuts. It's almost impossible to see how a body as reputable as the IFS would come up with such nonsense. It casually ignores that Scotland has been in relative surplus to the rest of the UK for most of the past decade and presumes that we would follow the disastrous lead of the UK's austerity agenda. Even with headline figures and a big reputation this report goes relatively ignored. People just zoning out of the relentless ponderings of doom and gloom and are just growing tired of all the negativity.

Out canvassing tonight in Perth. Grim, totally grim, as it usually is in the more suburban part of the city with a largely retired population. In the two hours I was out maybe found two committed Yes voters. One year to go, please not another year of such woe.

Saturday 21 September

Today's the day of the 2014 independence rally and for all its organisational shortcomings it is a massive success. The atmosphere was electric and thoroughly good-natured. It was in fact just a fantastic day out. This is the motivated Yes support coming out to play and just by being here it has revitalised our campaign. Numbers are everything and the police initially said that there was only 8,000 which was just so patently unbelievable (the much smaller rally had only 10,000 last year) that they had to quickly review the figure. In the end there were probably over 20,000 people making it the biggest turn out at a constitutional event since 1992.

Having been a veteran of those '90s marches and demos I detected the same sort of excitement and enthusiasm. There was also this really great sense that Scottish independence is taking on a much more mainstream appeal. The rally on Calton Hill was predictably too long and where there were some great speeches from Alex Salmond, Dennis Canavan and Nicola Sturgeon there were also some very unnecessary ones from people that most of the crowd would find difficult to recognise.

I was performing at the rally with a constituent of mine, Michael Yellowlees, we were in fact asked to close the event. Michael has written this song about independence based on his grandfather, a man called John Cullens, a hard-working activist and lifelong SNP member and independence supporter. John, from Highland Perthshire, was out for all of my campaigns and was always the first there and last to leave. The song is called 'Scotland is Ours' and it is a heartfelt tribute and a great patriotic song. I heard Michael first perform this at our constituency meeting and saw how this little song resonated with our support and could emerge as a fantastic anthem for our independence movement. I spoke to organiser, Jeff Duncan, who I knew from his days in the 'save our regiments' campaign and without much persuasion he put us on the bill. Had a great performance but disappointed that so many people had left bored with some of the more unnecessary contributions. Next year it has to be tighter, shorter and right to the point.

Sunday 22 September

Papers all about the march and rally, and most of it actually quite positive. It was either a 'rousing rallying call' or a 'forest of Saltires and lions rampant'. Reports cover the First Minister declaring that Scotland was a 'nation on the march' and how he suggested that we have an 'unrivalled opportunity to vote this nation into a new future of prosperity and equality – and to do so in a totally peaceful, civic and democratic manner.' The right-wing press were predictably less generous. Claiming that the SNP shared the platform with the 'hard left' and continuing to quibble about the numbers. Most, though, concluded that it was a good day for us and agreed that the numbers were impressive.

Labour conference at Brighton and Sunday is the traditional Scottish night. Usually there are television shots of Labour's English leaders uncomfortably doing the Dashing White Sergeant and tonight we had Harriet Harman only too happy to oblige. Amongst all the pas de basques, there was something a little bit more sinister on offer as Margaret Curran used her speech to call nationalism a 'virus' that has 'affected nations and done so much harm'. Almost unbelievable in its potential connotations she had thrown this verbal grenade in our direction the day after the rally, and with it has significantly lowered the quality of the debate.

On a more comical note, Margaret Curran also said that if we were successful it would mean the end of the UK Labour Party. Just thought of my many comrades who would be absolutely gutted at that possible outcome!

Tuesday 24 September

Believe it or not I'm at the Labour Party conference at Brighton today for an appearance with MP4 at the annual *Daily Mirror* reception! Greeted by my Labour friends with a mixture of 'what on earth is he doing here' combined with a curious, sneering mocking contempt, I take it all in good grace. Being a guest at their conference I had to be on my best behaviour and had to bite my tongue when speaking to Scottish Labour comrades, particularly with the 'virus' comments still kicking around.

Listened to Ed's speech on the way down to Brighton in Greg Knight's Cadillac (Greg is a Tory Government whip, our MP4 drummer, and an avid collector of vintage cars). Miliband dropped a bombshell about 'freezing' energy prices for a year, a commitment that will be met with bemusement from the energy companies and the press. He also raised the example of a Glasgow woman receiving lifesaving surgery in Liverpool as an example of the 'unified' health service and why we're therefore 'better together'. Really silly example as cross-border health care would continue whether we're independent or not as it is required by the European Union and as an example it meant absolutely nothing whatsoever.

At the reception we were on right after a contribution from Ed himself and I particularly appreciated the comical thumbs up he gave us as we took our position on the stage.

Our gig was actually great fun and we had hundreds of Labour delegates enjoying our cross-party rock. They particularly enjoyed our version of 'Things Can Only Get Better' and sang along lustily as if they actually believed it. It always amazes me that even in the midst of these bitter cross-party and constitutional exchanges there is still a little bit of space where we can all come together and put our rivalries aside. After the gig we hit the conference hotels and bars. Labour colleagues all trying to get my take on proceedings and doing their best to convince me that we had no chance. It was actually a fantastic night and it was good to get a few moments away from the battle and enjoy the company of those who we are now so bitterly engaged with.

Thursday 26 September

The 2001 census results were out today and we found that 62% of Scots say that they are exclusively Scottish with only 18% saying they are now British. The results seem to throw the whole issue of 'Britishness' on its head and would suggest that as an identity Britishness is on the decline to the point of practically disappearing in Scotland. I still believe that a sense of a British attachment exists in Scotland beyond these stark numbers and I further believe that these figures don't tell us the full story about the complex interweaving of our conflicting but complimentary identities.

This is something that particularly interests me and where identity issues have thankfully remained beyond the day-to-day indyref skirmishes there is a positive story to tell about Britishness from an independence perspective.

I believe that Britishness will remain an important feature in an independent Scotland and we will be keen to participate in building and developing new British institutions as an equal partner. I also wholeheartedly agree with the positive historic image of 'Britain' that the Nos present and I listen to them with great interest when they talk of Britain as the 'idea' that built institutions like the NHS and the welfare state. We also should recognise the positive contribution that 'Britishness' makes to Scottish cultural life. Our joint heritage and culture is something that we should all be proud of and it is something that will inform our future journey as we go forward as an independent nation.

For me Britishness is so much more than the usual confused and clumsy descriptions. It is in fact the sum of the 300 years journey we have enjoyed and endured on this island. It is what we have achieved and secured together in this partnership. It is about the great historic cultural achievements from the industrial revolution to our great rock and pop bands. It is about pride in our sacrifices in conflicts where we stood together and the collective sense of shame in our historic crimes of colonialism and slavery. Britishness is in fact the social union, and being British belongs as much to me as a proud Scottish nationalist and Scottish patriot as it does to anyone from England.

Where the referendum has absolutely nothing to do with 'Britain' it has everything to do with the political union of the United Kingdom. The referendum will be decided on how we determine our relationship with this peculiar political institution. Unionists try and conflate the UK state with Britain and Britishness suggesting if you vote Yes you would be voting to abandon 'Britishness'. This is, of course, nonsense and even impossible. We are primarily British by virtue of geography (most of us live on the island of Great Britain within the British Isles) but more importantly the institutions and joint culture we have built together is as much ours in Scotland as it is the rest of the UK's. You simply can't deprive a nation of its history like you can deprive it of the pound.

Independence can actually even reverse the decline of the idea of Britishness, a concept that is almost certainly on the wane. Britishness will exist in Scotland long after we become independent. In fact I think that it could well be enhanced with independence. With independence we will get the opportunity to define a new Britishness, one based on equality and mutual respect.

I would also be happy to see any number of shared institutions being called British and it could and should be the brand name of our new enhanced and equal 21st-century partnership. Who knows, maybe independence can give Britishness a new lease of life.

Friday 27 September
Opening of the Perth food bank this morning and I was asked to say a few words. I was already cautioned by the organisers not to make a political speech and I sensed their nervousness about my appearance.

The food bank, like most in the UK, has been organised by the churches in co-operation with the Trussel Trust. In Perth we have a very dynamic church community so the place was full with about 200 people turning out to see the keys to the building handed over by the provost – the council gifting the building to host the operation.

The Tories even turned up. The local Tory MSP, Murdo Fraser, and a smattering of Tory councillors were there, unashamed that food banks are a natural consequence of Conservative austerity politics. I, of course, respected the congregation, and had no intention of making a political speech, though was sorely tempted when I saw all those Tories sitting on the front row unaffected by this social disgrace being opened in one of the richest parts of one of the richest nations in the world. I simply noted that in my address and said I hope that it would not be a feature of our community for too long but feared it would be here for the foreseeable as we still have to bear the brunt of all of those (Tory) welfare reforms and continuing assault on our most marginal and vulnerable.

Cameron has also now ruled out a debate with the First Minister. Totally expected we have energetically got stuck in. The First Minister has called him 'feart' and there have been demands that if he won't debate he must stay out of the debate.

This is difficult for Cameron and he must have felt really compelled to do the debate, particularly when the alternatives are so uninspiring. He has said it is a matter for Scots, therefore conceding a role for him in the debate as Prime Minister of the United Kingdom. It is also a massive insult to the Scots who deserve the best possible debate which must include the main protagonists. Cameron has snubbed the Scots and has arrogantly walked away from a debate about our future. The Prime Minister of the UK will therefore not put the case why Scotland should remain in a union which has him as its leader. It looks just awful.

October 2013

Thursday 4 October

At the Scottish Parliament today to talk with Cabinet Secretary, Fiona Hyslop, about broadcasting and other issues as part of my Westminster arts and culture Westminster portfolio. Angus Robertson insisted that we make contact with our corresponding number at the Scots Parliament to feed into the final issues to do with the white paper. Where I wasn't holding out for all that a productive outing I was genuinely surprised how easily I secured the meeting, with two key SpAds thrown in for good measure. However, it quickly became clear that we are still writing the thing. I had this (obviously misplaced) impression that the White Paper was more or less complete and we were just doing the final few tweaks.

On broadcasting we still haven't decided the rather fundamental issue of whether or not an independent Scotland should remain part of the BBC. I was shown the two options under consideration (in or out of the BBC) and they were rather similar to the paper Fiona shared with me several months ago when we agreed that getting our position on the BBC was an imperative. My very strong view is that if we set up a distinct Scottish Broadcasting Corporation separate from the BBC it would be only too easy for the unionists to assert that we wouldn't secure programmes like Eastenders and Strictly. I made my views known on this and it seemed that Fiona agreed. This was to be decided by the cabinet (I didn't even know it was the cabinet that signed off on white paper inclusions!) on Monday and Fiona appealed to me to lobby John Swinney to secure support for this position. Scary stuff, and not in the least reassuring, particularly when I learned that the iconic issue of broadcasting would only get a paragraph in the white paper!

On the way out I asked the SpAd now in charge what are we doing about the lottery? Someone in John Swinney's office is working on it, I was not very reassuringly told. I therefore didn't even dare ask about creative industries policy and UK headquartered facilities such as collection societies, record companies and film interests...

Friday 5 October

Really hilarious piece about the comedian Kevin Bridges and his invitation to David Cameron's 'union' party on St Andrew's Night that's been doing the rounds with some of Scotland's entertainment community. In his refusal Kevin, aping Cameron, said 'my heart is saying f*** that and my head is saying Aye, f*** that'. Fantastic.

Monday 8 October

They've only gone and sacked Michael Moore! Total shock, which I suspect was a bit of a shock to Michael too. Michael is a thoroughly nice guy who has tried to pursue his position as Secretary of State as reasonably as possible. This has undoubtedly been his downfall. There is no room for soft soaping or positive engagement anymore in 'Better Together' and Michael's style is not what they are looking for in their dealings with us. 'Project Fear' has to be prosecuted with no prisoners taken, after all. They've replaced him with Alistair Carmichael, who has been the Liberal 'Chief' whip for the past few years. Alistair would like to think of himself as some sort of political bruiser but he is all bluster and bombard and about as scary as a wet blancmange.

Because of his engaging and more conciliatory style Michael probably hurt our campaign more than Carmichael ever will with his mock shrillness and famous short fuse. It was almost possible to forget that Michael was a Lib Dem and associated with a Tory Government, that's not possible with Alistair Carmichael. Having the post of Secretary of State for Scotland is the Liberals' most cherished and important position in Scotland so they have obviously thought hard about who should hold it. There is still the quad of the Prime Minister, Deputy Prime Minister, Chancellor and Chief Secretary (Danny Alexander) who have become increasingly concerned at the lack of activity from the Scotland Office and would seem are behind this change. So I'm afraid it's goodbye to reasonable engagement and hello bombast with the hopeless Carmichael.

Tuesday 9 October

The House of Commons finally returns from the long summer recess and it's business as usual, or as usual as it gets in this place. It's all reshuffle fall out and the scale of the reshuffle is actually quite extensive. On the Labour side it's reported as a 'cull of the Blairites' but the real story for us in Scotland is the end of meaningful Scots participation in the shadow cabinet. Jim Murphy and the pious Douglas Alexander are the only Scots left in the shadow cabinet outside the Scotland Office. The days when the Scots wandered the Labour cabinet like some sort of Caledonian colossi has now gone and it will never be back.

With the two Angus's (Robertson and MacNeil) on the terrace this evening and we come across Michael Moore. Looking at him it's quite clear that the stress of the last few days are etched on his demeanour and he is quite obviously upset at what befell him. We all said how sorry we were to see him go and he replied that he found all this love bombing from us Nats just a bit weird. Speaking to him I got to wondering if he might be upset enough to reveal a little about the machinations in better together, but suspect that he is too much of a gentleman for us to get much on that account.

Wednesday 9 October

Incredibly busy day today as I have secured a debate on the so-called 'hate vans' and 'go home' campaigns. It was very fortuitous as today was also the day that the Advertising Standards Authority effectively banned the vans and the campaign. Saw the Minister, Mark Harper, scurrying from studio to studio this morning taking some comfort from the fact that these vans were only banned for being misleading as opposed to be being banned for being full-on racist and offensive.

Since the full horror of these vans became apparent I have taken a lead role in holding the Government to account with a view to having them withdrawn completely. These vans have really appalled me and I let the Minster have it with both barrels and was very pleased with the way the debate went.

In the debate I said: 'I want people to imagine a situation where a van pulls a billboard through the streets, telling illegal immigrants to "Go home or face arrest". Just picture it. This is not 1940s occupied Europe; it is not even one of those National Front campaigns from the 1970s. This is the United Kingdom in 2013.'

It was noted that it took a Scottish nationalist to secure a debate on this issue and I wasn't surprised, after their disastrous intervention on this issue, Labour stayed well clear. It now looks likely that these vans will be withdrawn and I am immensely proud that I have managed to secure this little victory and have helped rid the streets of this obnoxious and disgusting campaign.

Had just sat down from this debate when I had to rush across to the main chamber for amendments I had tabled in the lobbying bill. My amendments were all about the House of Lords and the whole issue of securing a peerage on the back of a donation to one of the UK parties. Absolutely incredible in a bill that was at least notionally designed to end 'big money' in politics there is nothing to say about the House of Lords.

The SNP, Angus MacNeil in particular, exposed the cash for honours scandal in the last Parliament which led to a police investigation and the incredible spectacle of Tony Blair being questioned by the police. It was a massive hit for the SNP and Angus in particular and it was one of the main stories of the last Parliament. I argued that everybody who had been given a peerage should make an upfront declaration about all donations they have made to political parties. Needless to say my amendments didn't find much support, but they certainly found significant embarrassment.

Friday 12 October

In Aberystwyth to give the fraternal address from the SNP to the Plaid Cymru conference. Loved every minute of it and was absolutely thrilled with the spontaneous standing ovation that I received. Got all the usual calls from the Scottish media wanting to see my speech believing that I might say something that could be wilfully misinterpreted and used against us. I was almost sorry to disappoint them.

I was later on a panel with a variety of Plaid politicians discussing the impact of our referendum on the other nationalist movements across the UK. Wales is fatally compromised in its national question because of geography, as I found in just trying to get to Aberystwyth. There is practically no link between North Wales and the South. Plaid's strength is all in the North and they do very little in the big southern cities. Finding a 'Welsh' agenda therefore is a key part of any strategy in their going forward.

Plaid have started to learn a little from our experience mainly in talking up Wales' potential in energy and suggesting more and more that it could be an economic powerhouse given more self-responsibility. It's going to be hard for Plaid to replicate our success without starting to emerge as a national party and they have to be a bit more confident in their independence messaging.

Monday 15 October

Great story this morning about the fact we have attracted some 50 foreign diplomats to our conference in Perth. This is quite remarkable and shows the huge international interest in our referendum. You would think the unionists would even be happy? Not a bit of it. They responded in their default dreary and miserable way. For them we were selling a pup and a fallacy. They also couldn't help but suggest that we were too far beyond our station. How dare Scotland try and positively engage with international partners and explain what we are trying to achieve?

Tuesday 16 October

Shot a piece for *Daily Politics* today. No, not on the indyref, but on illegal downloading and fair recompense for artists. On my recommendation we shot it in the offices of the BPI surrounded by BRITs statuettes and Union Jacks. This is sure to antagonise and exercise my unionist colleagues when it's aired next Tuesday. I spent a lot of time working on the script but this will be forgotten about when they see the piece and the flags. Can't wait.

To confirm my British credentials I was also at Buckingham Palace tonight to meet the Queen as part of a group of MPs and MEPs. I'm firmly on the royalist faction of the SNP. The Queen is just as popular in Scotland as she is in the rest of the UK and it would be madness to approach the indyref with any proposal to get rid of her. There would also be the question of what to replace the monarchy with? Any elected President would quite rightly demand some executive powers and a say in our democracy. We work well as a constitutional monarchy and there is something attractive (if distinctly undemocratic) to have our head of state beyond the nastiness of our politics and media. It works. Just leave it alone.

Wednesday 17 October

Emerging story about the shutdown of the Grangemouth oil refinery. There was impending industrial action from the Unite union over a dispute over the shop steward, Stephen Deans, however, the union called it off at the last minute. The owners INEOS are still going ahead with the closure of the plant with huge consequences for production and oil supply. Saw the management on the evening news programmes defending this action and they seem to be using this dispute to pursue all sorts of different agendas. They are now going to negotiate with the workforce directly, over the head of the union, with the offer of diminished conditions and a no strike agreement. Using meaningless and nonsensical terms such as 'financially distressed' they are looking for Government intervention to get them out of a hole. This could be big.

Back in Perth for the start of the SNP conference tomorrow. Going to be a few big days. Looking forward to it.

Thursday 18 to Sunday 21 October 2013: SNP Conference

Thursday 18 October

Started Thursday morning with a great front page in *The Courier* stating that the SNP contributed some £3 million to the Perth economy with comment from me that I gave them yesterday. This is a very generous figure that I helped them 'finesse' based on the 2,000 delegates and guests spending about £450 each over the four-day period of conference. Went down very well, with the First Minister brandishing a copy of the front page in his opening remarks.

Delegates have warmed to Perth as a conference venue over the past few years and the city has increasingly welcomed the SNP. Inverness is now too small so we have become the unofficial conference venue. As the host association we try to make people as welcome as possible and engage our local businesses. I have contacted many of our restaurants and they now offer packages or deals such as a glass of wine or a free starter for delegates.

Headed down to the conference for the opening and it was a pretty low-key affair. Will be interesting to determine the mood of delegates and whether there is any concern or anxiety about our diminished position in the indy polls. Hung around to deliver the report from the Westminster group but because of an unnecessary debate over insignificant constitution issues we ran out of time.

In the evening it was pretty quiet round the city, even for an opening night. Just hope that some of that £3 million was being spent.

Friday 19 October

I'm on a fringe panel today for the Law Society of Scotland as our Home Affairs Spokesperson. When I accepted I thought it would be a typical low-key affair seeking to discuss a few legal issues round the indyref. How wrong I was. This has now been elevated as one of the key events of the conference fringe. The panel is me, former party leader, Gordon Wilson, and TVs ubiquitous pollster, John Curtice. Entitled 'Independence – on the cusp of a dream'. The Law Society anticipated some verbal fireworks and a genuine attack on the way the referendum was being conducted.

Also on the panel was Tasmina Ahmed-Sheikh who has been trying to get herself involved in almost everything recently. In advance I was getting calls from the press asking what I was going to say and I know that they were trying to wind up Gordon to say something controversial. The event was typically packed with standing room only with the press poised over their notepads. I spoke first and gave a rabble rousing, but on message, speech which seemed to disappoint my press friends. Gordon Wilson then went on to say that we must attack 'Britishness' so the press got their headlines and hadn't wasted their time. Total nonsense of course and so few in the party now accept this sort of stuff. Incredible that an attack on 'Britishness" is now met by embarrassed silence instead of cheers from party members. Shows how far we've come.

The highlight of the day was the Deputy First Minister Nicola Sturgeon's speech. Really was excellent. She spoke of Scotland in the event of No vote. That Westminster would 'turn the screw' and our devolved services would be under threat. Exactly what we need to do to help kill off 'more powers' in the event of a No vote. The highlight of her speech was a pledge to cut energy bills by £70 by taking out the 'green charges' from the bill and having these commitments made directly by Government. This puts us in the frame on energy bills with a workable commitment that could be made with independence.

Saturday 20 October

Always the big day with the First Minister's speech so Perth mobbed and everybody excited. But first thing in the morning I get a call from the Business Convenor, Derek Mackay, asking me not to push the remit back in the resolution on the Common Weal project. This followed similar requests from Kevin Pringle and the rest of the press and SpAd team last night.

The Common Weal is a left-wing think tank and offshoot of the Jimmy Reid Foundation and they present a vision of an independent Scotland from a left-wing/socialist perspective. It 'imagines' a new way for an independent Scotland to be run with big aspirational ideals about shared social ownership and Nordic-scale social services. How this is to be achieved is less clear but it would seem obvious that only through a mandatory policy of nationalisation and higher taxes could we secure these lofty ambitions. The 'programme' is set out in an 18-page pamphlet and a website. It is not therefore what could be referred to as a 'comprehensive' vision.

But yet, it has huge support in the party, particularly amongst the left and the trade union group. Many elements within the party are looking for something a bit more 'exotic' to support, anxious over what they see as an overly cautious approach to the independence referendum from the general Yes campaign. The thing is I have never met anyone on the doorstep who has actually said that they're not voting for independence because it doesn't seem left-wing enough. Usually they want to be reassured. Either about currency or the economy. This also blunts the idea of Scottish independence being an 'all' Scotland crusade. Where we have to appeal to Labour voters and talk up some big redistributive ideas we have to be careful not to knock middle-class voters off the other side.

The party leadership has also been relaxed (though privately critical) about the emergence of Common Weal and have let them do presentations to councillors and the MSP group. Such is its seductive appeal the SNP councillor group have even adopted its programme! Today they managed to get a resolution on the agenda asking the party to look at this proposal with an amendment stating that the party 'may wish to adopt this model'. No, we may not, was my response! I therefore made it known that I would remit this back to be looked at again.

The press team said that the resolution only uses words like 'may' and 'wish' and committed us to nothing. I was told that by remitting it back it could cause a huge row and instead draw unnecessary attention to the resolution. I then got the usual – the press would have a field day if I went ahead. I eventually backed down, very reluctantly. Now feel very disappointed with myself that I didn't push this.

The First Minister's speech was one of his best, using language that I hugely approve of with some fantastic attacks on Cameron's refusal to debate. I particularly liked the 'step up to the plate or step out of the debate' bit. He also started to inject a bit of patriotism and national motivation into the debate saying that a Yes vote in the referendum: 'will be, above all, an act of national self-confidence and national self-belief.' Spot on. He finished by saying of the day after the referendum 'we will wake up on that morning filled with hope and expectation – ready to build a new nation both prosperous and just… let us ask ourselves these simple questions: If not us, then who? If not now, when?' Great stuff.

He also revealed the date of the White Paper which will be published just before St Andrew's Day on 26 November, just hope it's ready. Ended the day with an appearance with MP4 at the conference ceilidh and revue, which I had organised and also compèred. After appearing at the Labour conference we thought it only right and fitting we should play for the SNP at Perth. My two Labour and one Conservative band colleagues were made to feel right at home and enjoyed the atmosphere of a party consumed in its constitutional agenda. The place was mobbed and had the good fortune to hear my debut on lead vocals on The Proclaimers' '500 Miles'.

Sunday 21 October

My only appearance at the conference lectern this morning introducing the culture resolution which was to be presented by me and culture secretary, Fiona Hyslop. Fiona said she didn't feel she should speak on the resolution as she had already delivered her Cabinet

Secretary's address the other day (a particularly good one) so I got someone else, Ross Colquhoun from the National Collective, to second it.

The National Collective are an online collective of young artists and creatives and they have been doing a fantastic job in promoting independence to young people and young artists in particular. They have developed a strong personality of their own and their insights into the cultural dimension of independence has been articulate, informative, insightful, and spot on. They have also enlisted most new artists and have helped make Yes the cool option in the indyref wars. Most young artists would now say they will vote Yes mainly down to the effort of the National Collective. It should come as no great surprise that artists will support independence. Being creative is all about imagination and nothing could be more exciting than imagining a new nation and the many possibilities that a new nation will offer.

In the afternoon we held a rally basically just to fill the time with the two hours we had left. It was a bit of a mess but we got away with it because of strong speeches from Alex and Yes leader, Blair Jenkins.

The presentation of the rally reached a low point when the obligatory TV star, who no-one seemed to know, couldn't pronounce the party president, Ian Hudghton's, name correctly. There was also a rambling introduction of our brand-new Yes app, the ingeniously titled 'Yesmo' that no-one will ever use. Blair Jenkins was particularly enjoyable using combative language that he has thus far stayed well away from. I particularly liked the bit when he said 'Vote Yes and we can say enough to the remote House of Commons and the ridiculous House of Lords: enough of the warmongers and the job-cutters; enough of the asset-strippers and the mortgage-flippers; enough of the welfare-bashers and the bedroom-taxers.' Way to go, Blair.

So where are we following our last conference before the independence referendum? We're still not seriously addressing the reality of our position in the opinion polls but there's something more important going on. There's a curious mixture of a true belief that we can win the referendum, merged with a defiance forged in the face of the battle with the Nos and the unionists. The party is looking around for a more determined and different approach (the Common Weal) but is also aware that we are in a complicated exercise of persuading our many reluctant fellow Scots. They also accept absolutely the leadership offered by Alex Salmond and Nicola Sturgeon and they accept that a cast iron discipline is required to take on our many detractors. In all I would say that it is like 'we have started so we will finish'. We may get beat but, by God, we will give this our best shot. And looking round at this lot here in Perth it will be a pretty good shot given.

Tuesday 22 October

Quite a day. On *Daily Politics* with the piece I had shot for the BPI. The BBC had put this up on their website first thing this morning and it looks great. Really pleased with the package and how it came across. The Beeb phoned me in the morning to say that I would be appearing with Labour MP Tom Watson in the interview. On air I had a good debate with Tom and we had a fantastic response. Tom later tweeted that I was 'a good man' who cares about music and bands even though he disagreed with me about copyright.

Later I spoke in the immigration bill. Truly dreadful piece of legislation that seeks to bring social services and housing into the Tories battle with immigration. Short term immigrants would be expected to pay for treatment and landlords would be effectively acting as immigration officers checking up on their tenants. This bill is a typical right-wing view of immigration. I was called quite early and spoke defiantly against the bill. I also reminded the House that the Scottish Government is in charge of health in Scotland and it would take a lot for the Tories to convince my colleagues in Edinburgh that these health measures are something that we would wish to pursue.

Wednesday 23 October

It's all about Grangemouth today. INEOS have announced that they are closing the petrochemical part of the Grangemouth refinery with the loss of 800 jobs. This has been building up for days and has dominated everything in Scottish political debate. Absolutely awful of course.

We had a statement in the House of Commons and everybody said all the right things about hoping there could be further talks and urging both Governments to help out and assist. That was until disgraced MP, Eric Joyce, got up and got stuck into the unions. Later saw Joyce in animated exchange with Renfrew, and Unite union-sponsored MP, Jim Sheridan. Couldn't help thinking that Jim should just get out the way and stay clear. Eric has already shown that he's prepared to go beyond standard Parliamentary engagement when it comes to exchanges with fellow MPs after having been arrested for 'sinking the heid' in a Tory MP in Strangers bar.

Monday 28 October

Where I can't get a PMQ, today I got a chance to question Cameron on his Commons statement on the EU summit. I told him the Scottish people were pleased he had found time to engage and debate with European leaders but wondered why he was being a big feartie in running away from debating with the First Minister on independence. We then had a rowdy exchange on keeping Westminster totally out of the debate. At the end he gave me a good-natured wink to show that he enjoyed the exchange. It's funny you would never have got that from Blair and certainly not from Brown. Cameron may be a Tory toff right down to his expensive shirt tails but he's a bit more human than his previous two predecessors.

Tuesday 29 October

First great scare story in ages today with Theresa May in Scotland to present a Government paper saying we couldn't properly organise and create security services. She goes further and says that an independent Scotland would be a security risk and that the rest of the UK would not share intelligence services with an independent Scotland. Almost unnecessarily over the top, the sheer nonsensical thrust of this report is verging on the embarrassing for the Nos. I had actually thought that the Nos were scaling down the scare stories but this shows that they are still prepared to pursue this type of nonsense when required. The Nos have actually missed a real opportunity because our plans for security services are, at this stage, practically non-existent. Had they been measured and reasonable, and asked the right questions, they would have found that they could have been kicking into an open goal.

Thursday 31 October

As the SNP group at Westminster it's always presumed that we speak on behalf of the Scottish Government on reserved issues when we get to our feet and speak in the Commons. If only! We can sometimes have immense difficulties in securing our government's view, and trying to get a line, never mind a considered response, is sometimes almost impossible. It is something that immensely frustrates the Westminster group and is the source of massive irritation.

Today is a classic example. After desperately trying to get the briefs on high speed-speed rail that is being debated today, we've taken to phoning our Ministers on their mobile phones to try and pin them down. Now we have had two conversations with the Minister and even at the point of voting on this critical issue we are not all that certain what the Scottish Government's actual thinking is. Eventually we vote for high speed two on the very tentative grounds that a UK Government Minister is coming to Scotland to talk about the benefits to our government tomorrow. Just hope she shows up.

November 2013

Sunday 3 November

Is the age of the scare story over? Fascinating article by Iain Macwhirter in the *Sunday Herald* today about the diminishing returns of the scaremongering campaigns. He highlighted the whole week's scaremongering agenda from the IFS report to Theresa May's threats about terrorism and summarised the unionist's week as – 'Scotland would be an impoverished and defenceless country infiltrated by al-Qaeda, shunned by Europe, barred from England, forced into deep cuts in public services and run by politicians who are economical with the truth'. He then asked if anyone was listening anymore and if the press and the Scottish Government could even be bothered to pick it up and retort?

People are now tired of this and there is scare story fatigue, even in the press. The demand for a more intelligent and substantial debate is now overwhelming and maybe the age of the great scare story is dead. If this is the case it leaves the No campaign with little to say. A year of saying 'the best of both worlds' and harking back to the founding of the NHS and victory in the Second World War won't cut it. Instead they will have to be more subtle in undermining the Scottish people's confidence and be more intelligent in creating their uncertainty. This could be a difficult few months for the Nos.

Tuesday 5 November

The emerging cloud of shipyard closures has started to come over the Westminster horizon. At a Westminster group meeting, Angus Robertson dropped the bombshell that Govan and Portsmouth were to close and thousands of shipyard jobs would be lost. Govan is of course iconic in the industrial fabric of Scotland. This was the place of the Jimmy Reid 'nae bevvyin' sit in and as a political symbol it is huge.

Shipbuilding is also a massive issue in the independence referendum and is probably one of the strongest suits that the No campaign can deploy. They can credibly claim that if we became independent the UK defence shipbuilding contracts would be lost. That's because the UK doesn't build complex warships in foreign countries, and in their view, we become foreign when we become independent. They therefore in a whole variety of leaflets say that 'separation shuts shipyards'.

The closure of Govan by the UK Government would therefore be a massive blow to the No campaign and deprive them of one of their main scare stories. Angus said that this devastating news would be delivered in a statement on Thursday but he had a question to the Prime Minister tomorrow and there is also Scottish Questions. We therefore discussed tactics and what he, and the rest of, us should ask. I asked who else knew about this information and if it would stay silent, fearing such news would obviously be leaked and get out to the press.

Sure enough, in the evening the news was breaking – but only that it was Portsmouth that was to close and Govan saved, but with some 800 job losses in Glasgow to go. The BBC claimed to have this an exclusive and were punting this hard. There was also the behaviour of the Glasgow MP, the erratic chair of the Scottish Affairs Committee, Iain Davidson, saying that the defence contracts should be awarded to Scotland but with a break clause allowing the UK to pull out if we vote Yes. He was actually suggesting that his constituents should be punished if they vote Yes. Extraordinary behaviour, even for him.

Wednesday 6 November

With the news of the shipyards already out, the statement on their future would be given after Prime Minister's Questions. Govan is indeed to be saved and even before the statement this was being trailed as a sop to Scotland and a concession to the No campaign. Scottish Labour MPs are also saying that this is a victory for the union and shows how we're 'better together'.

First, though, Prime Minister's Questions, and incredibly, neither Cameron nor Miliband raised the shipyards leaving Angus Robertson the opportunity to get in there first. Angus was very good and set it up nicely for the statement. There were then some 'robust' exchanges between our group and the Scottish Labour MPs in the statement and I stood with both the Westminster Angus's. This is a tough issue for us but the Secretary of State was very clear in his responses not to rule out Govan continuing to make UK warships in the event of a Yes vote.

Thursday 7 November

Still shipyards, and today it's taken up the road to the Scottish Parliament. All of the leaders' questions in FMQs is on the Clyde shipyards and Nicola Sturgeon, standing in for the First Minister, handled it perfectly. She quite rightly rounded on Scottish Secretary, Alistair Carmichael, brandishing a copy of a local Portsmouth paper in which he said that he believed the Govan work may still go south if we vote for independence. Nicola, in referring to this ham-fisted intervention said 'I thought his behaviour yesterday was shameful. He is the Secretary of State for Scotland. His job is to stand up for Scottish interests [but] he is quoted in the Portsmouth press this morning talking about taking jobs away from Scotland. That's disgraceful.' Quite. To Johann Lamont she said 'our shipbuilding industry is being downsized before our very eyes. That's the reality of the UK,' adding 'the threat to defence jobs in Scotland is not independence, it's Westminster and we're seeing that day and daily.'

The unionist parties in Scotland are in a sticky place with this. They can continue the scare tactic option and back Davidson's suggestion that the jobs could be taken away if the Scottish people vote Yes. This works with their uncertainty agenda but this would come across as determinedly anti-Scottish almost urging a future UK Government to 'punish' the Scots for voting Yes.

Monday 11 November

Forget the great constitutional wrangling today, there is only one story in town, and that is the fuss over the Duke of Wellington's head. Glasgow Council have decided that they will raise the plinth that hosts the statue of the Duke of Wellington on Buchanan Street in an attempt to stop the 30-year tradition of placing a traffic cone on its head. They claim that they have to remove the cones weekly at the cost of £100 a shot. Within a matter of hours this was met with a social media storm demanding that the plinth stays exactly where it is. In a display of great humour Glasgow people were not going to have this iconic piece of fun halted, and by the evening this campaign had forced the council to back down. Forget it, if you wanted to raise anything serious today.

Wednesday 13 November

Labour had an opposition day motion on the bedroom tax today, only some eight months after we in the SNP/Plaid group held ours. The bedroom tax has become this Government's totem of badness and is now considered the 'poll tax of our generation'. This was big and important stuff and you would have thought all MPs would be there to register their opposition to it; certainly all SNP MPs were. Throughout the day I noticed that I hadn't seen a number of my Scottish Labour colleagues and went to check the numbers who streamed through the lobby at the vote.

Standing at the door, with notepad and pen at hand, I was immediately approached by Tom Greatrex MP, who hissed 'pathetic' at me before angrily storming off. It was then that I knew I was on to something!

According to my very bad head counting I found that there were no less than ten Scottish Labour MPs missing from their 41 number, almost a quarter. When this was confirmed by Hansard I put all of this out on Twitter. Labour didn't just bring forward this resolution, they energetically ramped it up, parading round town and city centres with petitions. Writing to the Liberals to 'join them' in opposing this tax. The fact that so many of their number weren't there is going to be a huge issue for them and tonight this is looking profoundly embarrassing, particularly when this motion could have been won had they bothered to turn up...

Thursday 14 November

The rage about the 'great Labour no show' really kicking off this morning, and where this hasn't been picked up by the mainstream press, social media is going mad. People are genuinely angry that so many Labour MPs didn't turn up to their own debate in something as important as the bedroom tax. Labour feebly put something out about Labour members being paired with the Tories but this is only furthering angering those demanding what could possibly have been more important than this.

The truth is that this is a short week with the bedroom tax debate the only meaningful thing on in Parliament. Many members obviously saw this as a chance to have the week off and made an arrangement with a Tory opposite number. We in the SNP do not pair with other members and I'm feeling pretty good in demanding a three-line whip for our group last week.

Sunday 24 November

This week it is all about the launch of the White Paper and everybody is getting excited about what is to come. I, like nearly all of my Parliamentary colleagues, know next to nothing about its contents and like the rest of the Scottish public don't know what it's going to say. We have ceded all responsibility to Nicola Sturgeon and her civil service team and it has been a defiantly closed process. Our independence prospects rest on this document and it is probably our last chance to turn round the polls. What we do know is that it has 670 pages and 170,000 words making it a huge document. No country will have so much information outlining what is possible if it chooses its own constitutional destiny. I just hope that this paper can do it and that it at least engages people in the debate.

We also now know that if we vote Yes we will be an independent nation on March 24, 2016. The front page of the *Sunday Herald* says 'Independence Day' and an expectant nation is already purchasing the bunting...

The 'Radical Independence Campaign' held its conference this weekend attracting an amazing 1,000 or so people at the Marriott in Glasgow. Here, they outlined their vision of a left-wing, republican Scotland with added Scandinavia. With various appeals for more public ownership and attacks on the 'super-rich' their agenda was uncompromising.

The Common Weal's Robin McAlpine was there, of course, saying that 'This is a class conflict, this election. Rich people are voting No. So we've got to get everybody that's not rich out, and that takes work.' Yeah, right on comrade, and that's going to go down well in Perthshire and Edinburgh. I'm sure that there will be many independence switherers who will be observing this with nothing short of horror. Their endearing belief that Scotland is just waiting to get motivated behind a hard left agenda is almost touching in its naivety and they are going to have to calm down soon or they will really start to hurt the campaign.

Monday 25 November

It's the day before the launch of the White Paper and a sort of indy 'fever' has almost taken grip on the media this morning. In last minute jostling the Nos have been trying to lay as many traps and roadblocks as possible. Currency is of course the predominant one and they are relishing the fact that they control our plans for a shared currency as it rests on UK agreement. Yesterday Alistair Carmichael took this debate to a new height when he said that the SNP plan to keep the pound 'won't work' with Alistair Darling saying the SNP's plans to keep the pound looked like a 'non-starter'. Currency is probably going to be the key issue in the response to the White

Paper and it is probably round this that the early skirmishes of the White Paper will be fought.

Finally saw a copy of the White Paper when out on a joint meeting with John Swinney. John tantalisingly brandished a copy when we had concluded a meeting with union reps in our constituency and I actually declined to have a look. I will wait with the rest of Scotland until tomorrow.

Tuesday 26 November

Today will be one of the biggest, if not the biggest, day in the independence referendum so far. At last the White Paper will be launched. It is due at 10am from the science centre in Glasgow and something like 200 international media delegates have been registered. Been on a call with Edinburgh where we were briefed about some of its contents and given the lines we are to deploy. No surprise. We're to say that this is the biggest exercise in consultation that any nation considering its constitutional future has ever undertaken. That it's a blueprint for an independent nation and that we have answered all possible questions as posed by the Scottish public.

First, though, there was another desperate last minute pre-emptive strike from the UK Government this morning when they revealed that independence will cost each Scot £1,000. Awful stuff and predicated on the treasury doing some modelling on the IFS sums. Alistair Carmichael valiantly took this round the studios but it sounded tired and repetitive. Everyone just wants to see the contents of the White Paper and the media build-up has been very impressive.

At the launch. It was the briefest of introductions before questions and what could only be called a 'solid' and business-like performance from Alex and Nicola. Almost understated, Alex seemed to ignore most of the questions put and answered what he wanted. Impressive in its simplicity the whole presentation was straightforward and to the point. Lasting just over an hour the FM and the DFM took nearly all questions posed. Then there was the White Paper itself. Such was the demand to see it that the Scottish Government website crashed.

Within an hour I managed to see the sections I was involved in and it was all there. Felt a little bit strange seeing all this in such an important document. It actually looks great and reads well. An impressive, user-friendly document, despite my concerns and anxieties about this exercise, I found myself warming to it immediately.

Where there is little new it is an impressive consolidation of what has been said only with a new chapter on increased childcare provision. This is interesting. Childcare is devolved but the White Paper makes the case that the investment that could be put in could only be delivered by independence as any gain would be lost to the treasury. Clearly a pitch to the 'problematic' female vote, but very clever.

Within minutes the Better Together spokespeople were out trying to rubbish the document and even before they had any chance to read nearly any of the 760 pages it was roundly dismissed as a 'work of fiction' which failed to address the 'real questions'. Sounding almost churlish they were trying to talk it out before it had even had the chance to open its mouth.

The whole exercise had seemed to flatfoot the Nos and their response was nothing other than predictable and tired sounding. Alistair Darling just sounded angry whereas our spokespeople sounded positive, encouraging and authoritative. All the early skirmishes went a lot better than I ever hoped for. The UK news was full of the story and it dominated all the headlines all day. By the end of the day the launch had been judged to have gone well and I think that we handled all the issues and questions decisively and even with a bit of flair. A good day but sense that it won't be like this for long…

Wednesday 27 November

All about the White Paper today and everybody trying to digest this substantial document. The right-wing press are doing all they can to give the White Paper the worst possible reviews but somehow we seem to have held the ground on this so far. The main response from the Nos is of course currency, as we expected, with the usual stuff about an independent Scotland not being allowed the currency union we require and the 'what is the plan B?' stuff. The Nos are now beginning to get some muscle into their response and are raking round all the detail to try and find weaknesses. They also seem to be focusing on our childcare plans which suits us as this is part of the agenda that we want promoted. Where all the press reviews are typically awful they don't actually say all that much.

I was tipped off that I would probably get a question to the Prime Minister if I stood today, so duly obliged. We had decided that we would keep the pressure on Cameron on his refusal to debate with the First Minister, So I asked him – 'the Prime Minister has said that he would fight for his union with his head, heart and soul, but what we need to see from the Prime Minister is some guts. We now know the case for an independent Scotland and we know what his union looks like, will he now stop being a pathetic big "feartie" and get out and debate with the First Minister?' It was an invitation he declined in his usual way.

One UK Minister who had nowhere to hide was the Scottish Secretary who was debating with Nicola Sturgeon on a *Scotland Tonight* special this evening. In an encounter that could only be described as a political slaughtering, he was pulverised by the Deputy First Minister. In desperation, he on several occasions, did the one thing you never do in those situations and that was to appeal to the moderator, in this case the lovely Rona Dougall. It was a great fillip to us and gave us great heart. Nicola has emerged as one of the UK's top politicians in the way that she has handled the launch of the White Paper and this performance will only enhance her already considerable reputation.

Thursday 28 November

Tonight was the night of David Cameron's St Andrew's Day bash which has now famously been boycotted by several Scottish celebrities. This morning we learn that the Prime Minister himself isn't even attending! I cheekily asked a question at Business Questions enquiring why the PM had decided to snub his own event? With all the call offs and 'sorry I'm washing my hair that night' Downing Street have been playing down the event. Apparently Cameron is 'indisposed'.

Friday 29 November

News coming in about a bad accident in Glasgow. It's being reported that a helicopter has come down and crashed through the roof of the Clutha Bar in Glasgow city centre. The whole thing sounds horrific and there looks like there has been casualties. On going to bed the whole scene looks dreadful and this could well be a major incident.

Saturday 30 November

The true horror of the helicopter crash is becoming apparent this morning and it looks like there will be many deaths to report. The First Minister has been out in front of the media with the leader of Glasgow City Council in a very consensual response to this tragedy. This is St Andrew's Day today and there is supposed to be a number of street activities to coincide with the launch of the White Paper but this will be pretty much restrained now. I was also at our national council meeting in Perth today to deliver the Westminster group report but the meeting was very subdued with the emerging news from Glasgow.

December 2013

Sunday 1 December

Where the helicopter crash quite rightly dominates the news there is a little bit of room for the White Paper. We have now had several days to digest this weighty document and we are now trying to assess the impact of its arrival.

Having had an opportunity to have read the whole thing I really like it and even find it quite inspiring. It is a very well written document that is accessible and reasonably user-friendly. Will it shift the debate decisively in our favour? Probably not would have to be the inevitable but realistic response and assessment.

The Scottish Government seem to be satisfied with the reception to the White Paper and the response from the Nos has been typical and over played. We, of course, expected the press, the UK parties and all UK institutions to attack and seek to undermine our case but they have so far failed to dent the public's appetite to find out more about independence, and the more the Scottish people look at the case for independence the more they seem to like the prospects.

But at first glance the White Paper and its media aftermath has failed to budge support for Yes. For all its detail and clarity, it has not convinced sceptical Scots that the independence policy of the Scottish Government is a sound one. This is reflected in the first opinion poll following the white paper. *The Mail on Sunday* has a poll which shows support for independence at a disappointing 27%, the same figure as an identical poll taken in September. 56% of respondents said they would vote 'no', while 17% said they 'didn't know'. It's probably too early for opinion to shift following the white paper but with all the attention I would have hoped that there would have been a least a few percentage points moving in our favour.

Monday 2nd December

Really funny story emerging from the *Financial Times* detailing a list of complaints from 'senior Conservatives' about the performance of Alistair Darling at the helm of the Better Together campaign. It describes him as 'comatose', 'useless', a 'dreary figurehead'. They lament that he has 'never ran a campaign' and is treating Alex Salmond 'too gently'. It reports that Whitehall officials have prepared material for the pro-union case which has not been used by Better Together, 'for fear of being accused of running a negative campaign'. It concludes that they have to get Gordon Brown back or look at senior Conservatives such as the Scots-born, Michael Gove, or even Jeremy Hunt!

I have no idea what's brought this on and it seems to have come out of nowhere. If anything Better Together should be satisfied with the ways things have been going. They are way ahead in the opinion polls (even in the aftermath of the launch of the white paper) and their 'uncertainty' agenda still dominates way ahead of any campaign themes we have planted. Alistair Darling may not be the most dynamic figure in politics but he's not done a bad job in leading a fractious cross-party campaign. It's being suggested that this has been put about because Darling may be considering rejoining the shadow cabinet. Whatever it is, it is a presentational disaster for the Nos.

Later in the day there are all sorts of stories about desperate calls from Number Ten apologising to Darling for the comments and right-wing columnists and bloggers have got stuck in at the 'madness' of criticising Darling. This is getting good and Darling will undoubtedly be upset at the comments and attention.

Tuesday 9 December

The Scottish cabinet went on tour today to promote the white paper to civil society in the first of a white paper grand tour. In a question and answer session to 300 invited organisations the fear is it will always get ambushed. Happy to oblige was Ian Mackay from the

Institute of Directors in Scotland who expressed his 'unhappiness' and 'frustration' about costings. Surprisingly this wasn't effectively dealt with and allowed this intervention to be a major news story. Hope if we are going to continue to do this we have in place quick answers to easy questions.

Cripes! Boris Johnston supports the union. In an otherwise silly and predictable intervention he started talking about the F UK. No, it wasn't an unsubtle coded message but his own invention of the 'former UK'. I don't know why the Nos think contributions from the likes of Boris are helpful for them. Where he may be almost lionised in London he's seen as nothing other than an upper-class buffoon to most Scots.

Sunday 15 December

It's been revealed that Better Together have received donations worth £1.6 million since April. And surprise, surprise, all that money has come from Conservative supporters. What we can now say is that the No campaign is a Tory-led and Tory-funded campaign. Labour being very quiet this morning will be thoroughly embarrassed by this. The Conservatives are, of course, the most enthusiastic unionists but the closer we can come to demonstrating that the No case is a Tory case all the better for us. So thank you all you Tory millionaires who want to keep your union. Your money also helps us.

Thursday 19 December

Parliament up for Christmas and everybody heading home. Will there be some sort of Christmas truce and a goodwill to all 'men' for the festive period? Not a bit of it. Credit ratings agency, Fitch, out of the blocks with a 'warning' on currency. This was Fitch who lowered the credit ratings of the UK when we were told that independence would lose us triple A status. Merry Christmas to them too.

Friday 20 December

Launch today of Wealthy Nation. An independence-supporting group of libertarians, the right-wing and some Tories. About time. We will only win the referendum if it is seen as an 'all' Scotland project and includes all shades of political opinion and all parts of the political spectrum. I've already noted that I believe the leftist drift of the Yes campaign is starting to hurt our prospects and we are beginning to be perceived as a left-wing project. Hopefully this will help to start to address it and just hope that the party's left wing don't get stuck in or try to undermine this. The only thing is it looks like it's led by the highly erratic, Michael Fry. He is not what could be described as the most user-friendly exponent of conservatism and hope he doesn't put people off.

Sunday 22 December

Last serious day of news before Christmas and there's a great story in *The Sun on Sunday* about the 'rebranding' of No under the amusing James Bond inspired headline 'Doctored No', the *Sunday Sun* has a 'leaked document' with all sorts of 'secret plans' to relaunch the Better Together campaign. In some hilarious stuff it suggests changing their name to the 'knows' warning that saying 'no' is like saying no to Scotland. So 'Know' it is. It goes on to say that the negativity isn't working and they have to change the tone of their campaign. Somehow think the Nos or the 'knows' aren't going to oblige anytime soon.

2014

Referendum year. This is the year we choose. For half a century independence has been an ever-present feature in our political life. This year we decide whether it will become a reality.

January 2014

1 January 2014

Referendum year. In what will be just about the biggest year in recent Scottish history and it has barely started with a whimper. First there are the now traditional New Year messages. Cameron has stuck to his 'we want you to stay' pitch in which he was joined half-heartedly by Ed Miliband. None of the Unionist leaders have much new to say and with a quiet festive period news wise no-one seems to be listening. Alex Salmond also talking about our 'historic opportunity' but also curiously understated. Hope we're preparing to ramp it up when the festive period is finally concluded.

Sunday 5 January

We're back to the non-debate between the PM and FM this morning with an SNP commissioned poll which finds that 65% of Scots want a debate compared to only 25% who don't. Even in the rest of the UK there is a clear majority in favour of a debate. Not certain if this is in anyway going to change Cameron's mind but it is right that we keep up the pressure. Firstly, we can pick up on the hypocrisy when Cameron's Westminster's Government continue to deliver their analysis papers and secondly it reminds the Scottish people that it is Cameron in charge of the No campaign. Cameron made the referendum the centre piece of his New Year address and every time he opens his mouth on independence he will face this challenge for a debate.

Monday 6 January

Nicola Sturgeon giving what has been described as the first big indy speech of the year from St Andrews today. In a packed hall she put forward a clear pitch to Labour voters and challenged the No side to produce their 'white paper'. She said the 'No' campaign must set out a 'competing vision' of Scotland's future comparable to the one laid out in the White Paper with the familiar 'choice of two futures' theme. The Nos have been continually mocked and ridiculed with their failure to deliver any sort of 'manifesto' for a No vote and now that we have set out our White Paper there is going to be an increasing demand to get at least a steer about what a No vote will entail.

Wednesday 8 January

First PMQs of the session and Angus Robertson has a question. The half hour of questions had come and gone and Angus was still 'bobbing' when he was eventually taken. It was the usual stuff about refusing a debate and delivered without anybody really noticing. Then almost right after him came the unhinged chair of the Scottish Affairs committee, Ian Davidson, and he had the House in stitches. He made an appeal for Cameron 'not' to debate the First Minister because the Scots would not be receptive to a 'Tory toff from the Home Counties' putting the No case. Cameron, to his credit took it cheerfully and responded in the only way he could, by accepting it. In response he said 'I humbly accept that while I am sure there are many people in Scotland who would like to hear me talk about this issue, my appeal doesn't stretch to every single part.' Won't stop him effectively running the No campaign, though and Labour politicians like Ian Davidson campaigning for the right of unelected Tories like Cameron to be the Prime Minister of Scotland.

Sunday 12 January

Helpski! Seemingly Cameron has been in touch with Russia's Vladimir Putin to help him out in the independence referendum. The *Sunday Herald* has a front-page scoop featuring Cameron, Putin and Salmond all ominously peering out at the prospective purchaser. Seemingly, Cameron has appealed to Putin, as current chair of the G8 to assist in the independence referendum. Cue all sorts of Russian gags with the hashtag #indyrefski trending on Twitter. Some hilarious comments such as 'tapps afski' and 'from Russia with Gove'. Great stuff and again shows the humour in the indyref debate.

Monday 13 January

The UK Government has announced that it will assume full responsibility for the UK's £1.2 trillion debt if Scotland becomes independent. In what is a huge development the UK Government says it is doing this now in an attempt to avoid 'market jitters' from creditors nervous about what happens with UK debt in event of a Yes vote. This is exactly what we suggested in the White Paper and blows a massive hole in the UK Government's position that it won't prenegotiate or prepare for independence. What it means, at its most literal, is that we can now effectively walk away from our share of the debt and there would be nothing that the UK can do about it.

This now puts us in a very strong bargaining position when it comes to dividing up the UK assets. We have always said that we would take responsibility for our share of UK debt but this is a timely reminder that with debts comes assets. It is also important as it shows how quickly the UK Government will respond when the situation requires and it begs the question – if they can do this on debt why not do it on currency and EU membership? This is now the time to remind the Scottish people that we have a huge share in UK assets and start using this position to demand the end of the nonsense on currency sharing. Already sensing that we're starting to play this down and that we don't want to take advantage of this incredible new situation.

Thursday 23 January

It's the Cowdenbeath by-election today and we are going to get hammered. Labour have thrown absolutely everything at it wanting a result that would suggest that they've 'turned the tide'. Out and about I found all sorts of Labour Ministers and Labour students who had clearly been bussed in from England. Spent the day out and about in Inverkeithing, Rosyth and North Queensferry, places I know well from my time living in Dunfermline. By 7pm I had had enough and went home to watch a feast of indyref tele starting with my Perthshire colleague, John Swinney, appearing on *Question Time* from Dundee.

After that we were then treated to by-election coverage on both the BBC and STV. I put out a few things on Twitter suggesting that if Labour didn't get close to 60% then they were not going to have that fantastic a time, reminding them they almost got 50% at the last election and that we secured 28% in Cowdenbeath in 2007 when we won the Scottish election.

The final result gave Labour an 11% swing and we secured 28% of the vote. So a good but not entirely spectacular result for Labour. Another feature was once again UKIP lost their deposit but still beat the hapless Lib Dems, whose vote was so low that they were included in 'the others' in the result coverage. We also did something very clever, and that was to survey the constituency for independence finding a small majority for Yes. This stopped Labour credibly claiming that this was a vote against independence which is something they clearly wanted to suggest as much as any by-election win.

Saturday 25 January

Dreadful piece in the *Daily Mail* today about the so-called 'cybernat phenomena'. In an almost creepy exercise *Mail* journalists stalked and doorstepped online Yes activists before 'exposing' them on their front page. The evidence against looked pretty flimsy and seemed nothing more than I get in the course of any week online. The real intention of this campaign is to try and silence online critics of the union. The Nos more or less control the mainstream media and can easily influence what is included in their headlines, but they can't control the online engagement and comments.

We have successfully used online media to reach people we can't get because of our problems in being reported fairly in the mainstream press and the Nos are keen to present this as something intimidating and unsavoury. So far they have done this with a bit of success. This, though, just looks like bullying of their own and a clear attempt to silence the Yes online voice.

It's Burns Night and all over Scotland and the world there are Burns

Suppers being held celebrating the birth of our favourite cultural son. There has been the usual debate this year about whether Burns would be a unionist or nationalist and this has gained extra potency with the referendum. The unionists seem even more anxious this year to claim him as their own. I'm doing three immortal memories this year and we have been encouraged to enlist the memory of Burns into our contributions. The Nos let it be known that we were in for a treat this Burns Night by releasing the name of their newest supporter at a 'virtual' Burns supper at 8pm. We all therefore tuned in to find out who this was before being decidedly underwhelmed as it was none other than the Scots-born, but clearly American-sounding panto star, John Barrowman.

Sunday 26 January

Incredible opinion poll out today and we've narrowed the gap to an impressive 7% points. It is the best poll we've seen since our own (dodgy) poll of the late summer. It is the largest swing towards Yes recorded so far in the campaign and it actually seems to be pretty legitimate. It has found that support for independence has grown from 32% to 37% since September this apparent surge is accompanied by a corresponding drop in the No support by five percentage points from 49% in September to 44% currently. The poll also found that when the 19% who said they didn't know how they would vote were excluded, support for Yes is at 46% compared with 54% who said they would vote No. It got even better when the 'don't knows' were pressed further on their views on independence 'most likely' to vote, the results were factored into the equation and the pollsters found that support for independence stood at 47% compared with 53% in favour of No.

Beginning of a real feeling that things have been moving in our direction in the past few weeks. The White Paper has stood its ground and the real interest in it has seen a bit of a movement to us. Perhaps a sign of a real momentum? Have to wait and see with that one.

Monday 27 January

Still Burns season and we're at the Burns reception in the Scotland Office tonight to hear the 'lone panda', Scots Tory MP, David Mundell, recite the 'Dumfries Volunteers' to us. This, he maintained, showed that Burns was a unionist, etc – it was one of these nights.

We in the SNP group still turn up to these events but we feel increasingly like alien interlopers in the midst of this orgy of overwhelming unionism. I always tease them saying I'm only here to measure up the curtains for when the palatial Dover House becomes our embassy to the rest of the UK.

Wednesday 28 January

The Governor of the Bank of England is coming to Scotland to talk about a currency zone and our aspiration to keep the pound. This is being rightly trailed as significant and everyone is trying to second guess what he might say. We are obviously anxious about what's going to prevail particularly when the Nos sound so confident about his speech and how this will effectively kill off our currency plans.

First the Governor had breakfast with the First Minister and there was a jolly (well, as jolly as a Governor of the Bank of England can get) photo opportunity at Bute House. The speech itself contained very little that was actually new. He talked of the very obvious point that if a currency union was agreed there would be some ceding of sovereignty. He also gave the example of the eurozone and some of the issues in difficulties with that monetary union. What he didn't do was rule the idea out or even say it was a bad idea and you could almost feel the disappointment in No towers.

What he did say was that he would implement any arrangement that was agreed between the two Governments. Later on the BBC I saw Alistair Darling practically bursting a blood vessel attempting to convince some hapless TV interviewer that this was all over for the 'nats'. The Nos desperate to keep the currency uncertainty and are playing this for everything they've got. And yes, where it's unhelpful it doesn't make much difference and as dear old Alistair reminded us it's 'the logical and rational choice'.

Thursday 29 January

Supporting independence would be 'dishonouring the war dead who fought for the United Kingdom'. So proclaimed former Conservative Secretary of State, Lord Lang of Monkton, in a preview of a speech he will give in the House of Lords. In some truly appalling remarks he went on, 'for generations, Scots and English have lived alongside each other, sharing a British heritage. Would that not dishonour the sacrifices, made in common cause, of those who died for the United Kingdom, a nation now to be cut in two if the present generation of Scottish nationalists have their way? I earnestly hope not.' In truly outrageous remarks it is a massive insult to service veterans who just so happen to support our nations self-governance and independence.

On hearing the trailing of his contribution, the First Minister asked the Scottish Tory leader to disassociate herself from these remarks at First Minister's Questions which she, almost unbelievably, obligingly did. This did not deter them in the Lords where speaker after speaker backed Lang's remarks. In the evening the arch right-wing veteran Tory, Michael Forsyth, even rebuked Ruth Davidson for being a 'new' leader and falling into 'Alex Salmond's trap'. The whole spectacle in the Lords was almost comical in its serene surreal horror. I have no idea why the Nos thought exposing these very strange, other worldly people to the Scottish public gaze would help them. What it has in fact done is turn the House of Lords into an indyref issue and they will now become a feature of our case against the union.

Today was also the immigration debate final stages in which I was speaking. The immigration bill is a nasty, pernicious bill designed to meet the challenge of a growing UKIP in the polls. The bill also impacts on our NHS and housing sector so I had a number of amendments tabled to exclude Scotland from the provisions of the bill. As we debate the bill it emerges that immigration is now the number one issue that most exercises the British people. In Scotland it barely makes the top ten. In England it might be the number one issue but in Scotland we have an understanding of our particular demographic issues just as we also have a deep understanding of our history in welcoming immigrants. At the core of our approach is that lovely saying in Scotland – we're 'all Jock Tamson's bairns'. Indeed.

Friday 30 January

There are some places where debating the indyref is incredibly useful and others where it is highly unlikely to find any favour. As I found to my cost today.

I was asked to appear on the BBC Radio Scotland panel programme, Brian's Big Debate, from the private fee-paying school, Strathallan in Forgandenny, Perthshire. Heading in I presumed a debate under the BBC's usual standards of balance with a mixed audience of those supporting and opposing independence. After staying hello to my fellow guests and our host, the always affable Brian Taylor, we walk into the assembly room to record the programme. It was then that I realised that this was not going to be any ordinary 'debate'.

The audience was entirely made up of 5th and 6th year fee-paying pupils, a group who couldn't be more alienated from the whole prospect and idea of Scottish independence. There was absolutely nobody there from the general community to provide any sort of balance, contrary to what is actually required from the BBC.

After half an hour of negative questions and hostile contributions from the floor I casually ask if anyone in the 250-strong audience actually intended to vote Yes, and after a show of hands there were three in favour of independence. I then mentioned the rather obvious point that private schools like Strathallan weren't perhaps representative of the school community or young people at large, making them even more hostile up to the point of enraging them. Perhaps, on reflection, it wasn't my smartest move to alienate what seemed like the whole audience, but they were never there to be won over in the first place. I was also frustrated that listeners would think that this was coming from some sort of neutral venue with some sort of balanced audience. The Strathallan kids then went on to jeer practically all of my subsequent contributions and pull a variety of faces when I spoke. I couldn't wait to get out...

On leaving I was prepared to leave it all behind as a bad day at the office only to find my Twitter feed flooded by these pupils with their own particular take on my contributions. In the evening this descended into abuse and I was variously called a 'gimp' and a 'wanker'. I then shared these comments and just let them hang. We hear about 'abuse' everywhere in the debates around the indyref. Just surprised to find it so raw here.

Saturday 31 January

Woke up to find my Twitter timeline besieged with comments, mainly at first from those who were horrified at the comments from Strathallan. It also looks like the kids who had sent the more abusive messages were trying to remove them only to be caught by the 'deleted by MPs' site that catches any tweets removed from MPs timelines. In the afternoon the press start to get interested then some of the responses were starting to get ugly. The No trolls were trying to describe this as me getting into a Twitter 'scrap' with 'school kids' while others just were abusing me for highlighting the abuse in the most horrific, unrepeatable, ways. For the first time on social media I was genuinely concerned about where all this might go and just a little bit fearful for my safety.

February 2014

Monday 3 February

The Strathallan stuff showing no signs of quieting down today. The school has now issued a 'qualified' apology splashed across the front page of *The Courier* with the rest of the No press (practically it all) still trying to portray this as a fight between me and the school 'kids'. The story is reported in most newspapers and I am being pursued by a number of journalists. As far as I'm concerned I have nothing else to say and I am grateful for the apology and that is the end of the matter.

Later though I receive the worst online abuse I have ever experienced and had to block a number of people. It is actually quite difficult to conceive what would drive people to such fury. This demonstrates (as if it needed demonstrating) that online abuse transcends the whole divide and infects every side. Today, coincidentally, there is a trial of somebody who threatened to kill Alex Salmond with online threats. All of this will go unreported by the No-supporting press because their agenda is to characterise Yes as the bullies with an out-of-control following trying to silence the debate. They're just not interested in the abuse heaped on politicians and personalities on the Yes side because it doesn't fit into this particular narrative. It is, though, quite scary when you're on the receiving end of some very ugly and threatening abuse.

Thursday 6 February

Today we have our first debate in the House on independence for months and it is oversubscribed with interest. It is a three hour general debate on back bench business time and if we're lucky we might get ten minutes. I'm leading for us and am expecting the usual noisy response I usually receive from my Labour unionist friends when I get to my feet. This time I scripted a straightforward passionate case for independence with the intention not to be drawn on their incessant demand for detail. The debate soon descends into the usual acrimony littered with the usual bizarre contributions.

There was Tory MP Rory Stewart telling us that he loved us. Former Colonel, Tory MP Bob Stewart going on about 'devils in skirts' and Labour dinosaurs variously telling us we were liars and fraudsters. The best comment was from the Labour dinosaur Jim Hood, who said that he would still be against independence even if it made Scotland richer. A typical Scotland debate in the Commons.

I eventually got to put the Yes case after about an hour or so of No speeches. I had eight minutes. Almost immediately I got to my feet there was the usual points of order, aggressive intervening and attempts to shout me down. I completely blanked it out and made the speech of my life. At one point the whole Labour front bench were practically shrieking at me in contorted rage.

After I had finished I went up to the Labour whip, David Hamilton, and asked him what this was all about and why do they believe that people seeing this barracking and shouting down helps them? We had a 'lively' exchange and waited for the next Yes speech from Angus MacNeil. Angus was listened to with a little bit more courtesy and I saw the Labour whips trying to silence the many shouters and aggressive interveners, belatedly realising how bad this intolerance of the other side looks on them. An almost mad debate with some truly appalling contributions. The House came across as a nasty intolerant place that just couldn't bear to hear the Yes case.

Later in the day I put up my speech on my blog under the title 'the speech they tried to shout down' and got an incredible number of fantastic responses.

Friday 7 February

Looked into my blog stats to find that almost 100,000 people have read my blog or seen the video that has also now been circulated of my speech from yesterday. The whole thing has practically gone viral and the response has been fantastic. Even with our ten minutes we certainly came out on top yesterday and most people were appalled at what they saw of the behaviour in the House of Commons. The Nos clearly see the House of Commons as their resource and their antipathy towards us has backfired. Maybe we should try and secure more of these type of debates in the House of Commons.

Tuesday 11 February

Almost ironically after last week's debate we had the floor in the House today as it is our once-a-year opposition day. We thought long and hard about bringing another independence motion but decided against because of the overwhelming numbers against us. The No case would, even on our day, overwhelm us.

Instead we chose the topic of fairness and inequality and put down a motion with just enough in it to ensure that Labour couldn't support. We had decided to give the full day to the one motion anticipating statements and urgent questions. Only there weren't any, and we therefore had six hours of debate to fill, with only two speakers down to speak from outwith our group. It seemed that Labour had more or less chosen to leave our debate alone just because it was the SNP. We therefore started briefing that this was a disgrace particularly when we are being told that Westminster should continue to exercise the powers that determine most of our inequality. We also started to furiously scribble down speeches to fill the time. In the end of the day we therefore had one hour speeches from Angus MacNeil and Plaid's Jonathan Edwards, infuriating Labour enough for some of them to eventually turn up.

In the vote Labour predictably abstained, leaving us the opportunity to say that they couldn't care about setting up an inquiry to look at the effects of Government policy on poverty – their stated position. All in all, therefore, a good day at the office.

Late at night a huge story is starting to emerge. George Osborne is seemingly going to say that he is ruling out a currency union. If true, it could be one of the most dramatic moments in the independence referendum campaign. Twitter full of it already. Let's see what the morning brings.

Wednesday 12 February

All hell is let lose. It seems that Osborne is going to rule out a currency union in what will be the most significant escalation of the independence referendum thus far. Already we have been on morning radio repudiating this as bullying and making it known that if we don't get our share of the pound then we have no obligations in our share of the debt. This is also the first time that the UK has revealed that they would make life as difficult as possible for an independent Scotland and have therefore decided that they will no longer be amicable in any independence negotiations. We sort of always sensed that they would play this card, for the very obvious reason that they can, but I didn't think they would play it so early. They must be starting to get really spooked by the tightening in the polls.

Just before bedtime it was confirmed that they would rule out a shared currency. Tomorrow then will be the day when the independence referendum is probably forever changed and redefined.

Thursday 13 February

There he is, our Chancellor of the Exchequer, all but ruling out a currency union.

Even though we knew he'd do this it still seems to be quite shocking to hear this new escalation. In his speech he said that it wouldn't work, that it was unreasonable for the rest of the UK to take on this responsibility and that he couldn't propose this to the rest of the UK, because they could be exposed to the 'unacceptable risks' presented by an independent Scotland. Delivered in his usual expressionless monotone style, the dead pan delivery just added to the menace. It just came across as ugly and even intimidating. The pound that we thought we shared with the rest of the UK is not in fact ours at all. We would be excluded, and the rest of the UK would now do all it could to make life as difficult as possible for an independent Scotland. It was a crushing rejection of our case for a currency union and quite clear and seemingly unequivocal.

We seem to be almost unprepared for this and there is no immediate response and almost a temporary paralysis. Concerned that there would be the usual phone round for response I phoned our press office for the holding line to be told that Nicola Sturgeon would be appearing on *Daily Politics*. Meanwhile all the Unionist parties are all over the media gleefully predicting that it is now all but over.

Nicola's appearance on *Daily Politics* was steady, if obviously tense and tetchy, with Andrew Neil again and again determined to get an answer for a plan B. I see the first signs of a toughing this out and sticking to the existing line that the UK will be in a different frame of mind following a Yes vote. Just as I see the constant demand for a 'plan B' to be asked – ad nauseam. Later in the day, as predicted, Ed Balls and Danny Alexander also rule out a currency union – so that's all the Westminster parties together on this.

As part of her visit to London Nicola is also speaking at the UCL this afternoon, now with added press attention. By now the line is toughened up that this is a political statement from the Chancellor, that currency union is still our preferred option and that this is in the best interests of both an independent Scotland and the rest of the UK. Not too sure if this is going to continue to be sustainable as the unionist start to put some muscle into their 'you're not getting it' line.

Later in the evening Alex Salmond is drafted on to *Newsnight* and *Scotland Tonight* to shore up our position. Alex is as persuasive as ever and almost has me believing that the Government is bluffing! He is helped by following a bumbling Danny Alexander who almost does what he can to blow the Government's advantage. There's still lots of debate in this yet.

Friday 14 February

The great 'St Valentine's Day massacre' is how the cartoonist in *The Independent* saw it with the three UK 'chancellors' packing away their machine guns in front of a blood-splattered Alex Salmond portrayed as a Caledonian Mickey Mouse. Meanwhile, Alex himself is on morning radio now stating that this is all 'bullying, bluster and bluff'.

Since we started this process it was always presumed that this would be done in partnership and that we would both work for the best interests of our respective nations if we did indeed vote Yes. This morning I actually feel quite sorry, but also angry, that this will no longer be the way that the referendum debate will now be conducted. Yesterday marked the start of a new hostility and the first signs of an apparent intention of a rUK to damage an independent Scotland if we dare to vote Yes.

The only positive is that there appears to be an emerging anger that the Scots have been bullied and threatened by the UK Government and there is already some evidence that this is building up. Back in Perth this morning someone actually came into my office, clearly incensed, insisting that he was now a committed Yes voter after watching George Osborne and Ed Balls cosy up together.

It is possible that we can get through this if we can tap into this emerging anger and present the UK Government as an intimidating presence determined to bully the Scots out of choosing for itself and being denied what we thought was also ours. So far the UK Government have at least attempted to demonstrate reasonableness and partnership in the referendum but that now looks like it's evaporating quickly.

Still many turns to go and at this stage it's now over to the Scottish people to see what they make of this dramatic raising of the stakes.

Saturday 15 February

No stop to the currency speculation and where it now leaves everybody. There now seems to be a bit more of a hearing for a 'plan B' with 'sterlingisation' not being disparaged as much as previously. Meanwhile Stewart Hosie was doing a question and answer with the *Daily Record* still ruling out any consideration of an elusive plan B. I have to say I have absolutely no idea what the 'evolving' line is. The thing that frightens me is that I don't think anyone else does either. Jim Sillars meanwhile is over on the *Daily Mail* saying that we now need to propose a plan B and that should be our own currency pegged to the pound.

Sunday 16 February

Just as we thought that the sterling argument was perhaps dying down up pops the other indyref perennial, Europe. On the Marr programme, EU president José Manuel Barroso drops the bombshell that it would be 'extremely difficult, if not impossible' for an independent Scotland to join the European Union, immediately escalating the EU membership issue to just about the same stratosphere as sterling. Where he has said things like this in the past he has never addressed this so directly and equivocally. He said that 'a new state, coming out of a current state, would need to apply' and that the agreement of all 28 countries would need to be secured. Bizarrely, he used the example of Kosovo as what could go wrong. Now, Kosovo clearly isn't Scotland. We are already in the EU and Kosovo is a new state still seeking to assert itself after the bloody Balkan conflict. A worse example couldn't be given.

This is serious and already there is great joy amongst the No campaigners. What still mystifies me is how a nation with 40 years of membership could be kicked out of the EU and what happens to all the current arrangements, people and passports? Barroso is also a politician and there is absolutely no doubt that he has been put up to this from the UK. It's likely that he is helping London out so that he can secure his own position with discussions with Cameron on the renegotiations about the UK's treaty arrangements within the Tory party. This is all singularly unhelpful and coming the same week as currency it is almost as if we are under siege. If the unionists were wanting to destabilise our campaign in one sustained go then they couldn't have done it any more effectively than this. Everybody taking a deep breath and waiting to see what happens next.

The Sunday papers also interesting today as they try to dissect how the currency issue has moved the indyref support and which campaign is up and which is down. Surprising that so many have picked on the possible response and fallout of Osborne's intervention. There seems to be a polarising in the sides this weekend and the interesting issue will be where the many undecideds end up.

Monday 17 February

Big speech by the First Minister today billed as a response to George Osborne's currency intervention. It is actually vintage Alex and a fantastic, passionate rebuttal of the Chancellor's case. Made in front of a business for Scotland audience in Aberdeen it is shown as full on both the BBC and Sky News channels. Referring to Osborne's refusal of a currency union as a 'George tax', he demolishes the case that there wouldn't be a cost if a currency union was refused. The figure given is that it would cost the UK Treasury an extra £500m in costs on firms if plans for a currency union were rejected. He also stressed the indignation line expressing real anger on behalf of the Scottish people on being bullied and threatened. This seems to be in line with the growing mood in Scotland. Beginning to sense a real outrage about the joint Unionist attack on Scotland and Alex articulating that perfectly.

Ended my day at a business for Scotland meeting in Perth. An incredible turnout of about 80 small business holders from Perthshire. Hosted by Business for Scotland chief, Tony Banks, just down from the First Minister's speech in Aberdeen, it was an impressive evening, made all the more impressive by a presentation from BfoRS chief economist, Gordon MacIntyre-Kemp. BfoRS are securing incredible traction in the indy debate and now have about 1,500 members. Their website is about the most visited website in the whole indyref debate and they speak in a manner that business people respond to very well. I saw several of my more indy-sceptic constituents nodding their heads in agreement to what they heard and in the conversations afterwards they were really receptive to the case. I remember when Jim Mather first took the economic case for independence round a largely unsympathetic business community and how hard we worked on building the case. We are now beginning to see the rewards of all that effort.

Tuesday 18 February

Gordon Brown doing another of his 'big' speeches today, on pensions. The usual stuff on how this will cost us more and how dreadful all this would be if we were independent. The usual No scaremongering stuff. But why Gordon Brown? There could almost be no-one more singularly ill equipped to discuss pensions particularly since it was him that raided pension funds and offered our pensioners an insulting 75p increase. Again, it is addressed in front of a Labour for Union banner instead of Better Together. I think the Nos are just so keen to get Brown involved that they will let him talk on any issue in front of anything he wants.

Wednesday 19 February

I go to the BRITs practically every year as a guest of the BPI because of my interest in music issues and the fact I am the only former professional 'rock' musician in the House of Commons. Over the years I have picked up most of the industries' agenda in the House of Commons and led the debates on the creative industries and things like intellectual property. I also, to the chagrin of my MP colleagues, put together the only Parliamentary rock band in the world, the aptly monikered, MP4. The BRITs is the corporate music industry's big night out and it is immensely popular, watched by millions of (mainly) young people. Since its move from Earls Court to the O2 invited MPs are shepherded into a corporate box like some sort of political pen with a few journalists to keep us amused and on our best behaviour.

Usually it is just a good night out and a chance to meet up with old colleagues and the many friends I have made in the sector. Not this year.

In accepting the award for best British male artist on behalf of David Bowie, Kate Moss, in reading out a prepared statement from Bowie told us that he wanted Scotland 'to stay with us'. An incredible intervention that I almost missed because I was in a conversation with the BBC's Ian Watson. Everybody of course fixed their gaze on me as the only Nat in the village and there was a general 'did she really just say that' gasp of amazement.

Went down to the after-show party and all the talk was of the Bowie intervention with music biz chums reliably informing me that the cause of independence was now lost after the great man's intervention. The Nos aren't exactly bulging with glamour and star studded endorsements so this was a fantastic coup for them. Where Scotland's music community is overwhelmingly Yes, the UK's is, to a woman and a man No, in that general 'what have we done to upset you so much that you want to leave' type of way? And there is then a general feeling of satisfaction at tonight's turn of events.

Somehow end up being in the company of Tory chairman, Grant Shapps and the always affable, if irritating, Labour MP Stella Creasy. I think we just about manage to conclude that Bowie's statement is 'noteworthy'. Eventually find the BPI's chair, Geoff Taylor, and asked him if he knew that this statement would be made? Geoff had no idea, and no-one had thought to ask Kate Moss what was included from Bowie. So tonight the Nos got one of the best pieces of advertising they could buy and it wasn't even in the adverts!

On social media the remark is everywhere and Twitter went mad. The Nos predictably went on the abusive cybernat stuff as it started trending on Twitter but it in fact showed the funny side of the indyref at its best. Some really funny stuff started to come out and his songs were parodied under the hashtag #bowiescotland. There was 'Jock, I'm Only Dancing', 'Ziggy Played Stranraer' and my favourite 'The

Man Who Fell to Perth'. Fantastic stuff and really funny. Got no idea what possessed Bowie to get involved in Scottish independence but it actually turned out to be really amusing.

Thursday 20 February

The first opinion poll since George Osborne's currency intervention this morning and incredibly it shows Yes up. In a Survation poll for (of all papers) the *Daily Mail* it has Yes at 37% and No at 46%, last month the same pollster showed a No lead of 20 percentage points. This suggests that the Scottish people have responded very badly to the Chancellor's intervention. This is very encouraging. We now have to play the indignation card very strongly. The message should be that we will not be told from UK ministers and we will not be denied what is jointly ours. The Nos may have spectacularly backfired with the threats and the bullying and they might just have overstepped the mark in assuming the Scottish people would meekly fall into line in being denied and threatened. The next few days and weeks will be critical as to whether the Scottish people will continue to be outraged or whether they will start to get concerned about what currency we might eventually use.

Papers also full of the Bowie remark and it even featured on the front pages of several titles. Seems incredible that one small sentence from someone with no track record in the debate can secure so much attention, but that's the indyref debate for you. The rightwing press predictably majoring on the small number of abusive tweets that they've managed to find ignoring the fantastic humour that it's generated.

Friday 21 February

Quite a lot of response to the shift in the polls following the Chancellor's intervention. *The Guardian* quotes the First Minister saying: 'Most people in Scotland would feel that George Osborne insulted the intelligence of the Scottish people... The indications we have so far is that the joint enterprise between George Osborne and

Ed Balls has backfired on the two unionist parties in spectacular fashion.' Other details of the poll also show that only 37% of people believed the Westminster parties meant what they said on currency and that only 48% of voters wanted a currency union anyway. It's increasingly interesting how all of the high stakes interventions are playing out. So far it is playing out badly for the Nos and beginning to see us take more advantage of the growing grievance of what we are now directly calling 'bullying and threats' from Westminster.

Former European Commission Director General Jim Currie also has a few choice words about the comments made by Jose Barroso telling Holyrood's European Committee that 'I think he was unwise to express the opinion he expressed. I don't think he was correct and I don't necessarily think that opinion is shared either among all the member states or even necessarily the Commission.' He went on to criticise Barroso for comparing Scotland to Kosovo and said a better comparison would be German reunification, where 'the political situation required a degree of pragmatism' and 'East Germany was incorporated into the EU in a matter of months.' This follows rumours that Barroso is seeking to become the next Secretary General of the United Nations. Something he would obviously need some support from the UK to secure.

Monday 24 February

Almost by coincidence both the UK and Scottish cabinets are meeting within seven miles of each other in and around Aberdeen. Sir Ian Wood has produced a report on oil reserves in the North Sea and has made a number of recommendations about how we secure the most from this resource. Both governments are therefore here to try and win the high ground on this iconic indyref issue.

To win this debate the Westminster Government has to convince the Scottish people that oil is somehow uniquely a burden for Scotland that we are 'too wee' to manage it and we need the 'broad shoulders' of the UK to manage it on our behalf instead. Today they are promising £200 billion worth of investment forgetting that they have squandered this incredible resource since it first came ashore not too far from where Cameron is sitting just now. We have asked (provocatively) for the UK Government to apologise for wasting this opportunity and have again pointed to the example of oil funded Norway where its population are now all but paper millionaires.

The images also look dreadful for the Tory cabinet. They are in and out of Scotland, some on a private jet, allowing us to deploy our 'scare force one' quip. Cameron is on an oil field with the obligatory hard hat but was singularly unavailable to meet ordinary people. The Scottish Government in response is holding a question and answer session and doing all they can to engage with ordinary people. In a tetchy interview with STV's Bernard Ponsonby Cameron is challenged to meet 'ordinary people' and almost incredibly accepts an invitation to go in front of a panel of floating voters. In all, this has looked horrendous for the UK Government and Labour sensibly staying quiet on the visit. Don't know what Cameron was thinking about with this silly day trip but it has not played out well in the eyes of the Scottish people.

Tuesday 25 February

The cover of the *Daily Record* is hilarious, if also quite surprising, There's a picture of the UK cabinet with the headline 'scuttle off home to think again' with a memo to Cameron saying 'if you think Scotland will be taken in by a token charm offensive from your Con-Dem Government of elitists who hammer the poor whilst lining their pockets of their millionaire pals then think again'. The *Record* then contrasts the Westminster cabinet's 'stage managed' meeting with our Government's public meeting, which gave members of the public an opportunity to ask questions. The right-wing press are obviously more compliant but this is very bad for Cameron and adds to the now very thick tone that we have been patronised if not insulted. The debate about oil will go on and on but this week's visit has been an absolute gift with Cameron looking very foolish indeed on oil.

The latest in the series of indyref debates on *Scotland Tonight* is the main feature this evening and it is the clash of the female titans with Nicola Sturgeon going head-to-head with the Scottish Labour leader, Johann Lamont. This has been built up quite excitedly in the past few weeks and everyone associated with the debate is looking forward to it. It could therefore surely not disappoint? Well, yes it can, with the poor to non-existent moderation from Rona Dougall, it is reduced to a screaming match that does neither of the participants much favour. In an unseemly and high-octane non-debate Johann Lamont happened to mention that 'Scots are not genetically programmed to make decisions'. Think that's a quote that's going to come back and haunt her.

Wednesday 26 February

There's another bedroom tax motion in the House of Commons today and again it comes courtesy of the Labour Party. Our Scottish Labour friends are still sore about us exposing them for failing to turn up at the last bedroom tax vote and are now particularly sensitive about the issue. That's why I was there with my clipboard and pen to count them out as they came through the lobbies. Most of them didn't like it, but it was soon resolved with some good-natured banter. Some of them even congregated round the Aye lobby to wait and watch me concede that they were, in fact all there, as they were. That was until the Labour MPs, Jim Murphy and Tom Harris came through.

Now, Murphy and I famously don't get on. I reported him to the Standards Commissioner when I was first elected because there was a suspicion he was using Parliamentary materials for party campaigning, something clearly forbidden, and a charge he was later cleared of. He in response organised a coup to stop me getting the chair of the All-Party Music Group. Honours even then, or so you would think. But Jim didn't get over it and instead indulged in one of the longest Parliamentary grudges in Scottish political history, resolutely refusing to speak to me ever again. I then, usually just try to avoid him, and him me.

When he came through the lobby he muttered something at me which I didn't quite catch and I just said lightly in response 'nice to speak to you too Jim'. He then went absolutely berserk! Running over to me he was right in my face continually shouting 'fuck off, fuck off, fuck off' almost covering me in spittle. He then went to join his Labour friends standing at the other lobby. I went after him and asked 'what was that all about' and he did it again in front of his Labour colleagues even more aggressively. At one point I thought he was going to take a swing at me. He then stormed off leaving me shaken and furious with Labour MPs looking on in bemused horror.

I quickly convened a small group of fellow MPs including Angus Robertson, Stewart Hosie and Mike Weir and asked them what I should do. We discussed whether I should make a point of order or go and see the Labour Chief Whip. I decided I didn't want to make a public fuss but I didn't want to let it go either. Murphy is one of the Nos that consistently goes on about online abuse – apparently real-life verbal abuse and intimidation is alright – so I simply tweeted the encounter and it was soon round all the journalists and other MPs. Guido Fawkes put it up immediately and sought out the Labour 'witnesses' finding that 'they couldn't make out what was being said'!

An appalling incident and just shows a dreadful thuggish side to Scottish Labour and particularly this very angry man and his quite obvious unresolved issues.

Friday 28 February

As a regular air commuter I have a healthy contempt for nearly all things British Airways. Not today. BA chief executive Willie Walsh has come out and said that he is entirely relaxed about independence and can see benefits if we do indeed become an independent nation. His support is pretty much predicated on corporate self-interest given that he is more than aware that we would almost certainly scrap the damaging Air Passenger Duty tax in an independent Scotland. But he goes further saying that this could lead to more tourism, more spending and an expansion of our economy.Later in the morning he is joined by Ryanair's Micheal O'Leary who says pretty much the same things only with his own particular panache and style. This is about the first real endorsements that we have had from 'big business' and it is most welcome. Won't make much difference but we can always pull them out the hat when the Nos try and suggest we have no such big business support.

March 2014

Sunday 2 March

Almost a bit of a hiatus this weekend after the high-octane jousting over currency, Euro membership and big business of the last couple of weeks. With so much coming in so thick and fast it's been almost impossible to grasp your indy breath. Don't know how it will be sustained it if it's going to be like this for the next few months but things are certainly heating up to gas mark 11. Today there's a bit on the relative finances in the respective campaigns and it shows ours is extremely healthy whilst the Nos are looking a bit threadbare.

We of course have the Weirs, the SNP supporters who just so happened to win £126 million in the lottery. They have now promised to give Yes a seven-figure sum. At our group meeting last week, Angus Robertson, reported that we have already bought up most of the prime billboard signs in anticipation of this donation and these boards will be featuring all sorts of Yes messages in the course of the spring. It is just possible that we can outspend the Nos and after our last two Scottish Parliament victories we know how to get a high-profile visual campaign. It is encouraging then that we are seeing it reported that we might just beat them in the battle of the billboards.

Monday 3 March

First poll to show a dip in our fortunes since Osborne's 'sermon on the pound'. This one comes from STV one of the few media outlets that hasn't got a particular axe to grind with us. It found that 57% planned to vote 'No' compared to 32% intending to vote Yes. Most importantly it showed independence two points down from their last poll in December. Worse than that it found that Osborne's decision to reject a sterling zone has made undecideds 'more likely to vote No'. This isn't good, but not particularly surprising. Where it does put a dent in our claims that Osborne's intervention has infuriated Scots and driven them into the Yes camp there was always a sense that this could be inconclusive and in time drive people toward No. What it also shows, perhaps unsurprisingly, is that Osborne's intervention has shored up support for both the committed Yes and No supporters. We have just to stick firm with the bullying line and hope that indignation and a patriotic sense of pride can still come through. What is particularly strange about this poll is that it doesn't equate with what we are seeing on the ground, not just in Perthshire, but all over Scotland, people are posting big shifts to Yes. Maybe a rogue poll. We'll see as there are many more to come.

Tuesday 4 March

On the plane to London I meet the First Minister's special advisors, the always gregarious but something approaching world-weary, Geoff Aberdein, the FM's gatekeeper, and Stuart Nicholson, former journalist but now committed Nat SpAd. They are down in advance of the FM's *New Statesman* address in London. This is the next instalment in this week's series of big speeches. Alex has been making a few speeches in London recently knowing that such is the demand from the metropolitan press on all things independence he is sure to get an audience. The Scottish press will then always follow, worried that the metropolitan press might get something they might be denied.

Alex's speech was excellent, mainly for his observation that Scottish independence would boost the rest of the UK by creating a light balance to London's 'dark star'. He said that indy would boost the rest of the UK and that a strong and independent Scottish nation would 'benefit everyone – our closest neighbours in the north of England more than anyone'. This balances the dreary assessment of North of England MPs in the House of Commons this morning in yet another Westminster Hall debate when they as one decried independence with the usual predictable borders and foreigners nonsense, failing to acknowledge that a vibrant dynamic independent Scotland on their doorstep might even be a bit of a bonus for the North of England.

Tuesday 11 March

I'm a guest of *Gallery News*', Rob Gibson, at the press gallery lunch in the Commons today, and what a treat, Alistair Carmichael is the main speaker! A lot of journalists wanted to take a 'pet nat' with them to this speech but only Angus MacNeil and I were curious enough to attend. Alistair isn't the most gifted orator to ever address the massed ranks of the fourth estate but he didn't do too badly on the mandatory funny section at the beginning of his speech. It was then like a switch was turned when he got on to the meat of his lunchtime speech. It was the 'you cannae dae that, we're no gonnae let you do this' stuff with all the other messages of abandon and doom that was offered as the main course. He also restated his view that there is no such thing as 'Scottishness' just a silly thing to say which only makes him look even extra daft. What I think he is trying to say is that there is a commonality of interests across communities in the UK and that in some respects we are little different. In that he is correct but to try and suggest there is no such thing as Scottishness or Scottish values diminishes our sense of ourselves and just comes across as totally ill-informed and insulting. Alistair would be better to stick to the scare stories without indulging in the amateur cultural sociology.

Wednesday 12 March

GERS (Government Expenditure and Revenue in Scotland) figures are out today and they are expected to be bad with lower than anticipated income from North Sea tax receipts, contradicting some of the things we are saying about Scotland's relative surplus with the rest of the UK. But first, Mark Carney, is taking questions at the Treasury Select Committee on independence and the pound. After much negotiation we managed to get Stewart Hosie on the Treasury Select but he is of course just one member with the rest of the committee committed unionists. Mark Carney says that RBS may have to move to London and that an independent Scotland would have to guarantee deposits held in England by Scottish-domiciled banks under EU law. Carney has tried to stay above the fray on the indyref refusing to join in the unionist orgy of telling us what we can't do – directly anyway. He's walking a fine line now and am pretty sure he will eventually be bowled over to the No side and in time become one of their top advocates.

Then it was to those GERS figures and it's the First Minister himself doing the press conference, always a sign that something needs 'sensitively' handled. Alex describes our ongoing fiscal strength and addresses this new perceived 'deficit'. He says even without oil and this new 'deficit' we still outperform the rest of the UK outwith London and the Southeast. The Nos are typically overplaying this with some of their more outlandish claims starting to get into the 'too wee, too poor' territory. They also are still trying to say, again, that oil is somehow a burden and a curse. This does not play well for them. With a more assured response the Nos could severely damaged us today. They typically overcooked and they lost an opportunity to really hurt us.

Thursday 13 March

A fantastic opinion poll out today in the *Daily Record* from Survation and it's our best showing of the year and starting to reflect what we're seeing on the ground. It showed 39% plan to vote Yes and 48% No, when the don't knows were excluded it would give a result of 55% No and 45% Yes. Excellent stuff and shows that all the efforts of the Nos' 'fearful February' and the so-called 'dambusting' campaign have failed to have the impact required. Another very satisfying aspect of this poll was that it found that about a quarter of all Labour voters intend to vote Yes. This poll will alarm the Nos as they have thrown everything at us in the past few weeks and we're still standing, even gaining. Their big gamble is do they continue to try and scare people out of voting Yes or start to work up their elusive 'positive case'? The only solid ground they can climb on to is the promise of more powers and that is the territory I think they will now move on to.

First Minister's Questions today and it's all on the GERS figures. All three unionist leaders ask practically the same question and the FM is excellent in rebutting them. If they can't make a significant hit on the back of such opportunities they will almost certainly fail. Great stuff from Alex today and he even managed to get the *Daily Record* poll in.

Out canvassing again tonight and I could hardly find any confirmed Nos. I can't believe the turn around in our canvassing in the past few weeks and this is looking and feeling very good. The same thing happened in the lead-up to our victory in the Scottish Parliament when we were seeing something on the ground that wasn't translated into the opinion polls. Could this be the same? Well we will soon see.

Friday 14 March

David Cameron's back in Scotland. It only seems like yesterday when he was up here for the last day trip but here he is again addressing the Scottish Tory conference. Today he tells us we should listen to the concerns from big business and that it isn't all about scaremongering while clumsily trying to scare us at the same time. He compares voting Yes to 'picking a motor without an MOT' and that it 'isn't worth the gamble'. He ends with the 'this is a major life decision' stuff. Speaking at the half empty, almost otherworldly, Scottish Tory conference it just looks bad. Cameron still isn't certain how to deploy himself in the debate. He is torn between his general unpopularity and his clear ability to speak reasonably well on the union. Be interesting to note how he deploys himself next.

Fantastic day speaking at an event with young musicians and music workers in the Concert Hall in Perth. I opened it in the morning and in the afternoon they hosted a session on what independence would mean to the music industry in Scotland. They couldn't find anybody to put the No side (practically no-one in Scottish music will publicly advocate for a No) so we got the stage to ourselves without a dreary naysayer telling us what we can't do.

On the panel with me were two of the most interesting people in Scottish music, Mogwai's Stuart Braithwaite and Chemikal Underground's Stewart Henderson. It was a great panel with both of them making some fantastic points to a very receptive audience. We have this constituency sewn up because of the support from acts like Mogwai and Yes is most definitely the favoured option amongst Scotland's creative community. Before the indyref we would never have had panellists like this at a political debate and the young people that listened to the debate so patiently would have run a mile to avoid it. Just shows the way that the indyref has engaged so many new people to political debate.

Sunday 16 March

In what was a standard interview with the First Minister on the Andrew Marr show all hell breaks loose. Questioning the FM about Barroso's 'you'll not get back in' remarks, Andrew Marr offered his personal opinion on the issue by casually stating 'I think it would be quite hard to get back in, I have to say.' Alex, quite obviously bemused by this extraordinary intervention asked back immediately 'Is that an individual expression, is that the expression of the BBC?' Marr then seemed to backtrack, but it was out.

We have always known that the main UK Beeb interviewers are hostile to independence but yet they cover the referendum as part of the general UK news coverage. Some of the UK BBC interviewers make no disguise of their antipathy towards independence such as Andrew Neil and Jeremy Paxman but usually there is a pretence of impartiality. That seems to be all but thrown out today with that one intemperate remark. Social media immediately got stuck in and I suggested that Andrew Marr should just get his Better Together t-shirt out. I perhaps went too far when I suggested that there might be 'consequences' for Marr, meaning (which I thought was clear) from the BBC. Such is the tone of the indyref debate that this was picked up as being 'threatening'.

The party put out a press release accusing the BBC of breaching strict impartiality rules and suggesting that Marr may have broken the corporation's own editorial guidelines. The Beeb were having none of it though and immediately backed their Man.

Monday 17 March

Woke up to find my 'consequences' quote everywhere and learned just what a threatening intimidating man I am from my friends in the Scottish press. Sometimes you just wonder!

Tuesday 18 March

It's exactly six months to go till the independence referendum and today we will see the 'more powers' offer from the Labour Party as their Devolution Commission announce their plans. This is a key moment because if Labour come up with a credible offer they might just be able to enlist the devo-max majority that still inhabits the outer limits of the opinion polls of Scotland.

We listened intently to the morning interviews to try and get a sense of what was to come and knew that when Labour started to play it down it was going to amount to next to nothing. And nothing it most definitely was.

Torn by internal tensions their plans are a shambles. On first glance it looks like a watering down of their interim report presented last year with the removal of taxes like Air Passenger Duty. On closer examination the true scale of the compromise becomes increasingly apparent and their plans for income tax seem almost incoherent. They propose that the share of the basic rate controlled by Holyrood ought to be widened from 10p to 15p in the pound – accompanied by the ability to vary the rates paid by more prosperous Scots in the 'higher' and 'additional' income tax bands who take home more than £150,000 and pay 45 per cent.

In the few interviews on the launch of this proposal Labour spokespeople mutter something about not making Scotland a tax haven for the rich! In fact it means actually keeping us at a competitive disadvantage. These plans are an obvious victory for the 'no more powers' brigade at Westminster who famously threatened to boycott their own conference if a possible devo-max offer was concocted.

Later we see Johann Lamont on *Newsnight* and to call her interview a car crash would be to insult cars damaged in vehicular collisions. She couldn't explain properly how her tax plans would work and she muttered something about pensions which had nothing whatsoever to do with what she was talking about. I almost felt sorry for her and Gordon Brewer got stuck in showing absolutely no mercy.

Saturday 22 March

Today we are on 'hostile patrol' on the High Street of Perth. This is the term coined by former Lieutenant Colonel, Andrew Parrott, who now chairs the Perth and Kinross Yes group. Andrew is a fantastic character and his personal story just shows how far the Yes campaign has come. A veteran of Iraq and postings round the world for the British Army, Andrew is steeped in the culture of the army officer class but he is now a passionate independence campaigner. The 'hostile patrol' is in aid of the Labour conference which continues today in Perth's Concert Hall. Andrew's view is that we assert our ground and let the Labour delegates know we are here, and right enough, we observe the Labour delegates doing all they can to avoid coming into contact with our very obvious presence. There's also a fantastic turn out from our Yes supporters with about 20 turning up for this 'patrol'.

It perhaps wasn't so great in the conference hall itself. Johann Lamont's speech ends up being a bitter and twisted affair. She said the SNP would 'go down as conducting the worst campaign of mis-selling in history' and if that wasn't enough we apparently are 'running the most dishonest, deceptive and disgraceful political campaign this country has ever seen'. She verged on criticising Alex Salmond for being childless and accused John Swinney of dishonesty and of exploiting poverty-stricken Scots. Throughout the weekend Labour have presented themselves as the party of 'honesty' and self satisfyingly termed themselves as newfound 'socialists'. The Labour faithful loved all of this and lapped it all up. What the Scottish public will make of it we'll just have to wait and see.

Monday 24 March

Quite a few things as usual going on in the independence referendum debate but the most important thing today is what Kermit the Frog thinks. Apparently, the green muppet has said he is for keeping the union in an 'interview' with the *Big Issue*. This has now gone everywhere with Kermit jokes and banter on Twitter. Even the Beaker lookalike, Danny Alexander, joins in tweeting 'I am reliably informed that Beaker agrees with Kermit – Scotland is Better Together in the UK.' We in Yes can only take comfort in the fact that 'Miss Piggy' is for independence, seemingly she wants to be Queen of Scotland!

Tuesday 25 March

If Labour could sometime see how we operate on our shoestring operation at Westminster they would be much encouraged. Today is the budget votes and there's going to be a vote on the resolution to decrease corporation tax with Labour down to oppose. This is a trap for us, and right now we are looking it up and down before considering how we try and disarm it. At their conference in Perth Labour made much of the SNP's support for big business, we were even 'Osborne max' for our support in cutting corporation tax for 'big business'. They know that if we vote for our policy it would mean marching through the lobbies with the Tories. Hence the vote. I am very reluctant to oblige Labour and I put forward my firm view that we should abstain because this is a cut for the whole UK and our policy is about securing a competitive advantage for Scotland. Stuart Hosie, though, takes another view and he is our Treasury spokesperson.

I flag this up with our SpAds and ask them to think very carefully about the politics of this, meanwhile as our whip, I get down to the business of ensuring that my colleagues will back this vote with the Tories, regardless of my own reservations. Ten minutes before the vote we get the message that Alex Salmond has looked at this and in fact wants us to vote with Labour and against the Tories and our own policy! This is communicated to me from the SpAds office and it is unequivocal, apparently Alex does not want to face the rest of the campaign with Labour saying we voted with the Tories to support big business. I quickly assemble our group and communicate the revised (and total opposite) line. The group seem almost relieved about this and we now vote with Labour. They were just surprised to see us in the lobby with them but it meant we did not hear a cheep out them all night – if only they knew about the total reverse in what we were going to do minutes before the vote. Think we avoided a potential iceberg today just in time, but boy, do we need to tighten up how we respond to these big, potentially dangerous situations.

Wednesday 26 March

Yesterday I got a visit from the Government Deputy Chief Whip, Greg Hands, asking if we were going to call a vote on the Government's welfare cap. This is the measure in the budget that calls on the total spending on welfare to be capped at a £119 billion limit and cuts found if it's exceeded. Greg very much wants to test the Labour Party on this knowing that there are divisions in their Parliamentary group. I assure him that we will indeed be opposing and if the Labour left do not call the vote we most certainly will.

Labour have said that they support a welfare cap in most of this week's press and now it looks like they will have to vote with the Tories. UK Labour have been looking at the opinion polls and they know the cap is popular in the UK and they want to demonstrate what a 'responsible' Government in waiting they are.

This is particularly tough for our Scottish Labour colleagues. They have just spent the weekend telling the whole of Scotland that they are now back in touch with their roots. Adopting the word 'socialism' like it had gone out of fashion and Tony Blair never actually existed. We were once again the 'Tartan Tories' and they were the newly proclaimed tribunes of the people. Well, today, they will walk through the lobbies with the Tories in support of a Tory welfare cap which will significantly impact on the poorest in our community.

All day I gently tease my Scottish Labour colleagues asking which way these newly redefined 'socialists' would vote? In the middle of the afternoon Ed Balls defiantly confirmed that Labour would support the Tories and an hour later they voted accordingly. We did all we could to embarrass Labour with messages like 'the weekend socialists back to the day job voting with the Tories'. Later in the evening I put up a blog with the 30 Scottish Labour members (a majority) who voted with the Tories. After this was left to hang Labour just had to take the shame. A very bad day for them and this blows holes in their strategy to outflank us on the left and stop the haemorrhaging of Labour votes to Yes.

The only comfort for them is it looks like the Scottish press, predictably, are going to totally ignore it.

Friday 28 March

The Nos are having a crisis meeting this morning in response to the closing polls and the increasing view that this is a campaign in trouble. This news comes, almost unbelievably, from the front page of the *Daily Mail*; surprising, because the *Mail* is a paper that is almost rabid in its support for the No case. In the piece the *Mail* suggests that there are any number of complaints about Alistair Darling and that the negative case doesn't seem to be working, almost laughable in a paper that always seems to embellish all of those scare stories itself.

The problem for the Nos is there is nowhere to go. On Twitter I note that they have three options. 1) up the fear 2) up the fear, a lot or 3) go absolutely mental and ballistic, with the fear. The rest of the press are staying schtum on this and there is no response from the No campaign itself. Almost unbelievably everybody on the Yes side is sharing the *Mail*'s front page on social media much to their great embarrassment.

Saturday 29 March

Just when it couldn't get any worse for the Nos an unnamed Government Minister has only gone and said that 'of course there would be a currency union'. *The Guardian* has this splash and it is dynamite. The 'private admission' by the unnamed politician – who, it is claimed, would be involved in the negotiations with an independent Scotland is almost unbelievable given this huge trump card they hold over us with currency.

The Nos' panicky response only makes the matter worse as they talk about this 'unnamed source' and an 'off the record remark'. They are forced once again to tell the Scottish people they won't get something which they believe is already theirs – the very thing that is leading to their difficulties. It also demolishes their 'under no circumstances' case and regardless how much they now say there will 'definitely be no currency union' we will always be able to point to this and say this is what would actually happen after a Yes vote. Dreadful for the Nos and it looks like they will have to reconvene that crisis meeting.

This all falls on the ongoing Liberal conference so all the press are there in what would otherwise have been a singularly forgettable affair. Alistair Carmichael is paraded in front of the cameras to try and diss the story but curiously only ends up conceding that Yes might now win the referendum! They need to get this guy off the cameras as quick as possible. In the evening the Nos are beginning to see just how much this is killing their credibility and there are all sorts of headlines emerging in tomorrow's press. It's going to be another one of these days for the Nos methinks.

Sunday 30 March

The front page of *The Herald* is unbelievable with a Better Together boat going under the water with the simple one word headline: 'sunk'. *Scotland on Sunday* are out looking for the mole and there is a sense of the crisis level in the No camp going off the scale. Everywhere in the media there are No people commenting on where it's all going wrong. Alex Salmond is on all the major networks saying that the Scottish people will never again believe a word the Nos say. That this is all the work of Alistair Darling and their belligerence on currency is now revealed as nothing but a campaign tactic. This is a big moment for the Nos and they are not handling it well at all. Alistair Carmichael is once again dispatched from the Liberal conference but he still goes on about the possibility of a Yes win but he now adds just how unfair it is in that we are outspending them!

A couple of the right-wing papers pick up on this unnamed Minister who apparently hints that Trident may be traded for a currency union, but both Alex Salmond and Nicola Sturgeon quickly close that down by simply saying that getting rid of trident isn't a negotiating tool it is 'instead one of the main reasons why we want independence'. There is no good place for the Nos to park this and the desperate attempts just look bad as they are played out in the sitting rooms of Scotland.

In Catalonia at an independence event with future Catalan President Pere Aragonès, August 2013

Independence rally, Calton Hill, Edinburgh, 21 September 2013
(Photo courtesy Documenting Yes)

Independence rally, Royal Mile, Edinburgh, 21 September 2013
(Photo courtesy Documenting Yes)

With musician Michael Yellowlees after the closing performance at the independence rally, Calton Hill, Edinburgh, 21 September 2013

Independence rally flying the flag for Blairgowrie, 21 September 2013

At T in the Park, Saturday 12 July 2014

The 'Yes in the Square' cast at Blairgowrie, summer 2014

With the Dundee Yes Bus, summer 2014

At the National Collective Yestival, Perth, summer 2014
(Photo courtesy Documenting Yes)

My last Yes meeting in Dunfermline before the referendum, Friday 12 September 2014

With Dougie MacLean and Pauline Marshall following our Caledonia event in Perth, 13 September 2014

At 'A Night for Scotland' at the Usher Hall, Edinburgh, September 2014

Young Yes supporters at 'A Night for Scotland' at the Usher Hall, September 2014
(Photo courtesy Documenting Yes)

Independence rally, George Square, Glasgow, September 2014
(Photo by Peter McNally courtesy Documenting Yes)

Independence rally, George Square, Glasgow, September 2014
(Photo by Peter McNally courtesy Documenting Yes)

Polling day at last, 18 September 2014

April 2014

Tuesday 1 April

Hey, it's April Fools Day and of course the papers are all trying to catch us out with their not particularly funny and unremarkable spoofs. This morning the joke seems to be exclusively on the Scots and our referendum. *The Guardian*, the *Mail* and *The Independent* all have singularly unfunny and obvious 'April Fools' which pokes fun at the Scots with ludicrous, and in part, insulting spoof stories. When this is pointed out as perhaps part of a pattern we apparently lack a sense of humour by not joining in with the splendid wit of the hilarious metropolitan press. The thing is one of the spoof stories is about the Scots opting to drive on the right following independence. This was actually suggested as a 'real' scare story by Labour frontbencher, Andy Burnham, only a few short months ago. Maybe why we don't get these April Fools is that they are just too similar to the scare stories we're served up every day in the indyref.

Thursday 3 April

Oh dear! There's been a bit of a stushie at a Scottish Parliament committee. It happened when the CBI came a calling and seemingly it descended into an 'ill tempered encounter' with the economy committee. The CBI is led by the independence hating, Iain McMillan, veteran of the campaign against devolution but now much feted by the Nos. He speaks on behalf of the Scottish CBI but we're never too sure as to just how many businesses he actually speaks for and what sort of authority he has even within the group he notionally heads. We also (it would have to be said) just dislike him because he is the unionists' favourite business lackey. It's reported that the Tory convenor (Murdo Fraser) had to tell SNP members to stop 'badgering' McMillan, while Conservative MSPs 'rebuked' SNP members for 'ganging up and mob rule'. I think what really annoyed them was when SNP MSP, Mike MacKenzie interrupted McMillan's long winded negative preamble to ask 'have you any idea how long this polemic is going to continue because we do have questions.' If they want to see badgering and bullying witnesses into giving answers can I suggest they have a quick look at the silly Scottish Affairs Committee at Westminster. There they have it mastered it to an art.

Friday 4 April.

Margo MacDonald has died. One of the pre-eminent iconic figures in the independence movement, Margo had an almost unique status in Scottish politics. As an independent she was able to articulate her support for independence unhindered by party interest and she was also able to raise unfashionable causes passed over by others concerned about short term popularity. Margo was very kind and supportive to me when I first became involved in politics and I was always grateful to her for the advice she gave me. I was genuinely upset when I heard the news come in even though I knew she had been very unwell recently. The tributes came in thick and fast and even those from the Nos were very sincere. This is a political figure we will all miss.

Monday 7 April

It's Scotland week in the US and as usual it's getting much more attention in Scotland than it is in the US. Tartan Week, as it used to be known, is Scotland's opportunity to shine in America with a big set-piece procession up 6th Avenue in New York. I am a veteran of many 'tartan weeks' and they are great fun whilst also doing a great deal to promote Scotland and make useful political links. This week, of course, it is taking on a much greater significance with the antagonists in the indyref debate determined to make their mark.

The First Minister is in the States doing what he can to secure jobs for Scotland but he is also there to put the case for independence. Over the weekend he gave a speech which sort of sums up our international pretensions when he said that Scotland should be a great nation but not a great power, an interesting concept which challenges the Nos' view that Scots want to be part of a 'strong' nation. In his speech Alex said 'I want to look today at the contribution an independent Scotland will make to the world... For most countries, greatness can only come from influence, not force, from soft, not hard power, from enlightened self-interest, not self-interest alone.' Interesting theme and I hope he picks this up further.

Tuesday 8 April

We awoke this morning to the incredible news of 'cataclysm' following independence. This comes in the form of an intervention by former Defence Secretary, and former head of NATO, Lord George Robertson, who said that independence would be 'cataclysmic' for the Western world and would even threaten the stability of all we hold dear. In a speech at the Brookings Institute in Washington he said that 'the forces of darkness would simply love it' whilst 'the loudest cheers for the break-up of Britain would be from our adversaries and from our enemies'.

Where we thought that the scare stories couldn't get more bizarre George Robertson has managed to take them off the scale and make them global. You can sense at once that the Nos are profoundly embarrassed at this mad rant and their silence is deafening with nothing coming out from them in support of these utterings. This follows the week when most of them agreed that a more positive campaign was required. Instead we get this 'cataclysmic' nonsense. All day there has been nothing but mocking of these comments, especially the 'forces of darkness' stuff, and 'cataclysmic' was even trending on Twitter!

Over the weekend there had been a call for more Labour peers to get involved in the independence debate. If this is going to be the quality of their intervention, then yes, more of them, please.

Friday 11 April

It's the first day of our spring conference today, our last get together before the independence referendum. We meet with the party in great heart following the progress in the opinion polls and the apparent disarray in the No camp. This weekend it's more of a rally than a conference and such is the cast iron discipline in the party there is absolutely no chance of anything detracting from our intention of presenting a positive vision of an independent Scotland.

Nicola is the main attraction at conference today and in what was a fantastic speech she actually had people almost close to tears in the audience. Her main pitch was to Labour voters who we are 'love bombing' this weekend in a continued attempt to recruit them to our cause. There were many references to 'we are going to win' and she said that Trident would play no part in any negotiations saying 'I'm fed up protesting against Trident. I want to see the back of Trident' and 'we'll be in the removal business' when we become independent. Nicola is now a politician at the top of her game and is much respected across Scotland from all sides. She is also the future of the SNP and reassuringly the Scottish people now know that we are more than just Alex Salmond. When the other Scottish parties are so poorly led we are extremely fortunate to have Nicola Sturgeon in our ranks.

Saturday 12 April

Still at Aberdeen at conference and the whole place is buzzing. Speak to a few journalists who seem to be almost infected by the enthusiasm and energy in the conference centre. After the empty seats of the other spring conferences we can not cram any more people in and this must be the biggest spring conference ever held in Scotland.

If only the stuff from the stage warranted this audience. Before Alex spoke there was a rally and it was all just a bit cringeworthy. For some reason we got the same anonymous, annoying, 'celeb' from last conference, and he still didn't have a clue who people were. This followed the financial appeal from one of our MSPs, Mark MacDonald, who fancies himself as a bit of a comic. Unfortunately for him he's about as funny as Alistair Darling with a headache. Next up was a preview of playwright, Alan Bissett's independence play, *The Pure, the Dead and the Brilliant*. Where it might work in a theatre it was just wrong here and when he got into criticising the royal family and the First World War we were starting to get into hostage to fortune territory. Angus Robertson then got up, reading from a hastily drafted speech, saying practically nothing. Thank goodness it all only took half an hour.

Alex was just brilliant though. In a further pitch to Labour voters he said a Yes vote was not about him, the SNP or the wider Yes campaign it was about the future of Scotland. He reinforced the momentum is with Yes and said of the No campaign that 'the more the people of Scotland hear the case for No, the more likely they are to vote Yes'. He then went on to accurately describe the Nos as the 'most miserable, negative, depressing and thoroughly boring campaign in modern political history'. He said that 'they are already out of touch with the people and are now losing touch with reality.' Alex is a master of pitching speeches and he did this to perfection today. Everybody went away more than happy and up to the fight.

We are certainly in a better place than we were when we packed up our conference in Perth last year and the enthusiasm amongst our membership is almost frightening in its commitment. There is a real belief that this can be won and there is great encouragement being taken with the mess in the No camp. Everybody feels the momentum and the mood shifting. I don't know if this will be seen as the high point of the independence campaign for us but it certainly feels great just going through these weeks. I'm almost getting carried away with all this too and when you feel that this is all just possible, it really does feel like something else.

Tuesday 14 April

In what would have been the now usual dreary day trip to Scotland by yet another Tory Secretary of State the Defence Secretary, Philip Hammond's visit exploded into something quite extraordinary and heartening. Addressing the defence dependent work force at Thales in Glasgow, lecturing them as to why their jobs would be gone in the event of independence, a young worker called Danny McGee got to his feet and bravely said to the Defence Secretary, 'I feel aggrieved that you've come up here and seem to be threatening that our jobs will go.' This was picked up on all news networks and seemed to perfectly sum up the 'we will not be told' attitude that has emerged recently amongst the Scottish electorate. Hammond, clearly shocked, didn't know how to respond, just giving the story extra legs. Later in interviews this was described as 'emotional blackmail' and Danny McGee was put in front of the cameras to further explain, if not exactly cogently, 'It just seems to be that attitude and perception of the No campaign, that negativity. It felt like a direct threat, it felt like strong-arm tactics and blackmail, when he brings your family into it.' In an environment that couldn't be more hostile, the Yes campaign has just found a new hero.

Not content with the Defence Secretary, Scotland was also pounded today by no less a figure than the fantastically titled 'First Sea Lord of the Admiralty' with another broadside of woe. In a flotilla of negativity the First Sea Lord was joined by other very important UK defence figures, Generals, Air Field Marshals, and the like to 'warn' the Scottish Government that our plans to rid Scotland of Trident would cost billions of pounds, sour relations with the rest of the UK and leave the country 'deeply resented'. They have even fired off an 'opening salvo' by writing to Alex Salmond to say that his policy would cast a 'dark shadow' over Scotland's reception on the world stage – hardly the Charge of the Light Brigade. But hey-ho, these guys are very much backroom generals.

The Scottish people may take seriously lectures from many self-important people but they are unlikely to take lectures from these increasingly ridiculous people and their 'Better Together' orchestrated message. If anything this is part of the No 'background noise' that is doing nothing other than irritating the Scottish people. The sooner these people get back to playing with their expensive shiny toys the better it will probably be, even for the Nos.

Thursday 16 April

Our favourite business organisation, the CBI, has been flushed out and it is a massive scalp for the pro-independence group, Business for Scotland. It has been forced to declare its hand and has notified the Electoral Commission that it will be an official backer of the No campaign. This now allows it to actively campaign for the Nos and it can now spend £150,000 on campaigning in the four months leading up to September's referendum. Already businesses have notified their intention to leave, both Tony Banks, chairman of the Balhousie Care Group and leader of Business for Scotland group, and Martin McAdam, chief executive of Aquamarine Power, announced they would now be leaving the CBI. Others have indicated their anger at the decision and it seems that the CBI hasn't even bothered to consult its dwindling band of members. Every time they now pronounce an opinion we can just say that they are a No organisation and every pretence of trying to be a some sort of representative body has gone. The hapless CBI Scotland boss, Iain McMillan has effectively killed off any chance of the CBI playing any sort of useful role for the Nos. Again we must thank him for his efforts.

Saturday 19 April

The CBI story still rumbles on with further companies and organisations deciding to quit the now No-supporting business group. Some had to, such as Scottish Government organisations like Scottish Enterprise and Visit Scotland. But Scottish Television have also left with SE saying that the 'CBI should have remained impartial and merely asked pertinent questions of both sides.' Another take aim at your foot and fire exercise by the Nos and just shows the scale of the mess they're in.

Sunday 20 April

'Scotland on the brink of independence' proclaims the front page of *Scotland on Sunday*. In what is perhaps the most significant opinion poll yet No is on 52% with Yes on 48%. It's from ICM and in a paper that is not particularly well disposed towards the case for Scottish independence. This is a fantastic poll and coming, as it does, with five months to go, the momentum is now clearly with Yes. The poll found another few interesting things too. Seemingly, there is now a majority for Yes amongst Scots-born voters, it's only when those born from outside Scotland are factored in that we start to fall behind. *Scotland on Sunday* are trying to suggest that the referendum may be down to 'English' born voters but even amongst them we are registering almost 30%.

There isn't even an attempt at a response from the Nos who must now be watching events with increasing despair. More and more it is beginning to feel like we can do it and the change in the mood is almost tangible. This poll will only encourage our already motivated support and will do nothing other than depress the No campaign. We need to stay at about here for the next few weeks and hope that the No campaign continues to dissolve. Great morning.

The next billboard from Yes is also revealed today. One word, 'Can', with a 't' on the end crossed out. Fantastic image and one that emphasises the hope and optimism in the Yes campaign. This is going to be some week.

Monday 21 April

The *Daily Mail* really have it in for Alistair Darling. Today they go for him again and almost suggest that he is personally responsible for the collapse in No support. They report that there are others lining up to take his place but they must be Labour – a sort of 'wanted, someone to lead crisis hit national campaign, Tories need not apply'. The Nos of course can't replace Darling, even if they wanted to, that would take their 'crisis' to 'meltdown'. Other than Brown there are no other senior figures who have any sort of currency amongst the Scottish electorate, but such is their desire for a 'prince across the water' to come forth and rescue them they will put it about that there might indeed be such a person.

Alistair Darling has failed as a leader but they are stuck with him and now have to make the best out of a pretty bad situation. The first thing they have to do is sit him down and try and make him a bit more appealing. His media performances have ranged from angry to apoplectic, this from a man that regularly won the most boring politician of the year award. To reinvent him as this angry, agitated, fountain of doom just looks really bad and I'm pretty sure that Scottish viewers are put off by the way he comes across in interviews. I don't know Alistair at all. Even though he and I have shared the same workplace for the past 13 years he has barely said a word to me – to him, I'm just an insignificant oiky nat. What I observe though is this aloof, diffident, even shy, figure who is just uncomfortable in this role. This is a problem because the Nos' current crisis is as much about leadership as strategy and they really have to start to involve the Prime Minister.

Having the UK Prime Minister as a semi-detached observer is just mad. This contest is about who should be ultimately in charge of our nation – a UK PM or a Scottish FM – and no-one can put forward the case for the UK better than the man that currently inhabits the role. Cameron is also about the best advocate the Nos have and he can convincingly put a passionate case for the union in a way that few other Nos can. He also comes with the authority of office. His involvement now might also galvanise the UK's response and indicate that maybe at last they are taking this referendum seriously. They have to figure out how to use him or their leadership crisis will just intensify.

Friday 26 April

The CBI have only gone and announced that it is seeking to cancel its registration with 'Better Together'. In a highly embarrassing move they are now trying to suggest that the registration was a mistake made by a junior member of staff! Described variously as a 'farce' and a 'cock-up' there is no comfort they can take from this. In a move that they have defended to the hilt up to the point when their position became untenable they even describe their decision to register with the Nos as 'an honest mistake'. The whole business case for the Nos has been compromised by the ineptitude of this almost chaotic organisation and their attacks on our campaign will always be blunted by this incredible gift to us.

Saturday 26 April

The CBI 'farce' still goes on today with the announcement that the hapless Scottish chair, Iain McMillan, will stand down at the end of the year. This has just been about the most inept episode in the short history of the No campaign and most of their credibility amongst business organisations has just about collapsed.

Monday 28 April

Putin's back, and this time it's us that's clutched in the paws of the Russian bear. Apparently the First Minister has talked of 'his admiration' for Vladimir Putin and how he has 'restored the country's pride' calling him 'more effective' than how he is often portrayed in the West. Predictably this has opened up a new Eastern front in the indyref wars with the unionists and press jumping all over these remarks with glee.

The FM made these remarks in *GQ* magazine in an interview with former Number 10 supremo, Alastair Campbell, just as the Russians got down to the business of annexing Crimea. They have been variously described as 'both disgraceful and dishonest' and 'insensitive and ill judged'. It is most definitely a curious contribution from the First Minister. Not only does he make these bizarre comments about Putin he also feels the need to praise Nigel Farage, of whom he says 'he is having influence beyond his significance so you have to admire that… I have a sneaking regard for anyone who takes on powerful establishments.' So, just as we have been trying to totally set ourselves up as a bulwark to UKIP-ism Alex is praising their leader! It would seem that Alex was sucked in to speaking favourably about world leaders by Campbell and it looks like he just couldn't help but oblige. None of this is helpful and a rare mistake from the FM. The press are going nuts and it helps keep the real indyref business of the day off the front page and that is the First Minister's speech in Bruges on Scotland and the EU. In what is (a now overlooked contribution) Alex says an independent Scotland would be an 'enthusiastic, engaged and committed' member, contrasting that with the less active and 'sullen' approach of the rest of the UK. Not entirely sure what Putin made of this contribution...

Wednesday 30 April

A new pro-union group has been set up. The imaginatively titled 'No Borders' styles itself as a grassroots campaign to deliver the 'emotional punch' that has thus far been missing from the official Better Together campaign. There's a website and a song, the rather dreadful 'Flowers of the Union'. This was felt to be so newsworthy that a big puff piece featured on *Newsnight*.

This has infuriated similar No groups who feel aggrieved that they have not similarly secured such favourable coverage. We have therefore determined to find out a bit more about our new musical unionist friends, and this being a campaign conducted with a new generation of online Yes inquisitors it did not take long to unearth a few gems. Apparently this 'grassroots' campaign is a project funded by former Conservative donor, the multi-millionaire, Malcolm Offord. We also discovered all sorts of London addresses and front companies. This is a 'grassroots' organisation for multi-millionaires which wants 'no border' except for the UK of course. A daft intervention which has the potential for much embarrassment for the Nos.

May 2014

Thursday 1 May

There doesn't seem to be any sign of Putin fatigue as all three party leaders lead on this at First Minister's Questions. This has now been running all week and I think a few of us would almost prefer to be taken to the gulag than have to listen to another mention of this now notorious interview.

The full *GQ* interview is available today and it seems that our over-excitable FM also had things to say about our drink culture (a nation of drunks, he apparently said, even though he didn't). He even had a pop at Obama! Looks like this is just going to run and run as it offers the great opportunity to extend one of the great No themes; the denigration and personalisation of the First Minister and the conflation of him with the whole Yes campaign. This is something they have invested strongly in and there are signs that it is working with many people on the doorstep stating 'Alex Salmond' as the reason why they are unsure about the Yes campaign. I somehow think we won't be getting any more of these sort of interviews before the referendum. If this has achieved anything it is probably the end of the conversational interview for a long while. Maybe a good thing.

Friday 2 May

The Nos are a bit more encouraged with the latest YouGov opinion poll which is out this morning as it has the gap at an impressive 16 points with them on 58% and us at 42% when the don't knows are stripped out. What this does conceal is that even with YouGov, the least favourable pollster for independence, there is a contraction of their lead. The *Daily Mail* are putting this 'increased' lead down to Putin even though most of the polling was taken before the Putin story broke. The Nos are desperate for a bit of comfort from the polls and are grasping at this one with both hands even though it is still showing the trend towards us. There is no doubt that the Nos are still ahead in the polls but it can't be more than 5% and their continuing chaotic campaign will only ensure that this is a trend that will continue.

Saturday 3 May

Cameron's not happy with the No campaign. He's made it clear that he wants to get out a bit more in the campaign particularly with all the talk of him having to resign if there is a No vote. He still won't debate but he will now embark on a number of high-profile visits to Scotland to appease criticism that he has kept away. Downing Street are saying that he 'wants to underline he is a national leader and stress what Scotland can achieve by remaining part of a strong UK'.

The 'How do we deploy Dave?' stuff is just nonsensical. He is the Prime Minister of the Union that they're hoping to save! No-one can argue for his right to do that better than the man that currently inhabits that role, and if this referendum is about anything it is about who should ultimately run Scotland – is it the UK Prime Minister or the Scottish First Minister?

Sunday 4 May

The *Sunday Herald* has only come out for a Yes vote, the first time in this campaign that any newspaper has come out for independence. In a fantastic, even beautiful, front page designed by author and artist, Alasdair Gray, this is enthusiastically greeted by Yes supporters everywhere. This is a significant moment as no national newspaper has backed independence since the temporary dalliance of *The Sun* in the early 1990s.

The editorial is fabulous, explaining their reasons for endorsing Yes saying 'there is nothing simple, clean, or clinical about ending a union that has endured for better than three centuries. Nevertheless, having considered the arguments, the *Sunday Herald* sincerely and emphatically believes that the best outcome is a vote for independence.' It goes on to say that the referendum was a choice between 'a bankrupt political structure' and the chance to 'remake our society in a more equal, inclusive, open and just way'.

There are stories of the newspaper running out and even some conspiracy theories of shops refusing to stock the *Sunday Herald*, and it indeed takes me three papershops to track a copy down. I've no doubt that *The Herald*'s circulation will be through the roof today with many Yes supporters wanting to keep a copy for posterity. Great morning and another very important moment in this campaign.

Monday 5 May

Papers still full of the decision of the *Sunday Herald* to back a Yes vote and speculation about whether *The Sun* will join it. In February, Rupert Murdoch tweeted: 'Let Scotland go and compete. Everyone would win' with many believing that this suggested that he might support independence. Backing from *The Scottish Sun* would be incredible as it is the highest-selling daily in Scotland with a circulation of over 250,000. By comparison, *The Herald*'s circulation is less than 25,000. *The Sun* does come with baggage after Leveson, and if it did back indy there would be the usual stories about Salmond pandering to Murdoch. But this would be all worthwhile as it would undoubtedly secure greater traction to the Yes campaign.

Tuesday 6 May

Pensions has been the staple of the No campaign for the past few weeks but today they seemed to have scored the most incredible own goal. The silly Scottish Affairs Committee drafted in pensions minister, Steve Webb, to give some further ammunition in their campaign against 'separation' only for him to instead give us a real gift.

On being asked about the State pension he said that we had 'accumulated rights' and that pension amounts would remain static adding that 'citizenship is irrelevant. It is what you have put into the UK National Insurance system prior to separation... that builds up to a continued UK pension under continuing UK rules. They are entitled to that money.' You can almost hear the air being sucked out of the Scottish Affairs Committee room as this sunk in. What he in fact confirmed was that the state pension would be safe in an independent Scotland and that the scaremongering was just all hot air. Another central pillar of the scaremongering agenda has again begun to quake.

Thursday 8 May

A fantastic letter in both the Scotsman and Herald today from the lottery winners and Yes donors Colin and Chris Weir in which they make an appeal for the 'smear' campaigns and 'personal attacks' to stop. This move comes after some appalling comment following their donations to the SNP, which they say 'poison' the referendum debate. The couple went on to say that certain politicians were 'targeting' them, hinting at Alex Johnstone, the Conservative list MSP who has previously said: 'While it's the right of every individual to do whatever they wish with their money, the SNP are clearly taking advantage of these people'. Making things worse he even felt obliged to attack them again saying 'this letter goes some way to proving my point, and I hope they didn't come under any pressure to write it.'

Saturday 10 May

After a week of speculation about Cameron's future in the event of a No vote a more solid position has emerged today. He has now said that he will not resign if there is a No vote. This follows claims by some Tory MPs that he would have 'little choice' but to go if the Union is lost. In what sounded like special pleading Cameron said: 'It is not about my future it is about Scotland's future.' Saying it was the right thing enabling this vote to go ahead. He said 'the vote is about whether Scotland stays in the United Kingdom or separates itself from the United Kingdom. It is not about my future.'

Some journalists have also been asking whether a No vote would mean Alex Salmond's resignation. That is probably a little easier to clear up as it would be almost inconceivable that Alex would want to stay on in the event of a No vote. Alex has already stood down once as party leader and it would be unlikely that he would want to go on having been a First Minister and delivering the referendum. We also have a ready new First Minister in place with Nicola Sturgeon to lead us into the next Scottish Parliamentary election. So where Alex's future is probably straight forward I don't think it is similarly the case for Cameron if he tries to remain in post.

Sunday 11 May

After expressing their unhappiness about how they've been 'targeted' I suppose the best way that the SNP lottery winners, Colin and Chris Weir, can hit back is to give the Yes campaign even more money. Today they announced that they are to give a further £2.5 million to the Yes campaign. The Nos are typically apoplectic and upset about how our campaign is funded by one donor. Maybe they should have kept their mouths shut when the Weirs were wondering what to do with their winnings.

Monday 12 May

Alistair Darling has been 'effectively dumped' as the leader of the No campaign proclaims the front page of the *Daily Mail* this morning. With quotes from Tories saying he has the air of a 'middlingly competent accountant' and was not the 'big figure' needed to lead the Labour charge. It reports that Douglas Alexander has been drafted in to reinvigorate the Better Together campaign. Their leadership issues just get worse and worse and it is now approaching chaotic.

Another fantastic Yes meeting tonight in Perth's Royal George Hotel which I chair and have arranged. I wanted another big Yes event in the city and managed to secure some fantastic speakers including Pat Kane, Derek Bateman and Tasmina Ahmed-Sheikh. The numbers turning up to these meetings just get more and more impressive and we had over 200 turning out tonight. Where most people are already Yes inclined what these meeting do is make their support more secure and also enlist them to perhaps go out and campaign. Tonight we must have signed up a further 20 volunteers, ready now to hit the streets and campaign for independence.

Wednesday 14 May

George Osborne's back today as the 'bad cop' of the indyref double act with 'good cop' Cameron. In front of the silly Scottish Affairs Committee he once again repeated the familiar line of 'no ifs no buts, there will be no currency union'. He even went further when asked about the possibility of 'sterlingisation' where we use the pound without agreement with the rUK. With that he put forward all sorts of tragedies that would befall us claiming that we would actually run out of hard cash by using another nation's currency.

He even said that we would lose our own Scottish bank notes if we pursued this approach. Our banking sector would also not survive and average mortgage payments would increase by more than £5,000 a year. Sitting next to him was top treasury civil servant Sir Nicholas Macpherson agreeing with everything he said and even embellishing the points if he felt the Chancellor wasn't menacing enough. Osborne must rank as perhaps the most unpopular Tory in Scotland but yet he is put up as the scare-master in chief. He actually does the role quite well and because he has the civil service on his side it does actually feel quite intimidating. It's all nonsense of course and I'm not sure what the Scottish people feel about this approaching apocalypse.

Osborne is also digging himself into a rather large hole. As he said himself there is 'no wriggle room' in this. What will probably have to happen is that he would have to stand aside in any negotiations with an independent Scotland as it would be almost impossible to have someone so defiant in his view sitting opposite us when we have to get down to the real business of getting a deal.

Thursday 15 May

Speaking at Cambridge University Union tonight in their independence debate. We took the decision that we wouldn't participate in English-based panel debates for the very obvious reason that people in England don't have the vote and it is not an effective use of our time. There are exceptions, though, especially when there is the possibility of media attention. We had first passed over the Cambridge Union event but came under pressure from Yes Scotland to participate, so it's now left to me to board the train to Cambridge. It is in fact a great evening and I spoke with Michael Gray from Business for Scotland against Michael Forsyth and Jim Wallace. Got the train back to London with Michael and he's on top form. Recalling stories of my Perthshire predecessor, the flamboyant and colourful, Nicky Fairbairn, and Michael's efforts to get the Stone of Destiny back to Scotland.

Friday 16 May

A Survation poll has shown that a third of Scots are more likely to vote 'No' to independence if they thought Alex Salmond would be Prime Minister. This comes the same week that Jim Sillars said that Alex has become a 'liability' to the Yes campaign. This poll comes as no surprise and is something that is regularly raised on the doorstep. The personalisation of the No campaign round Alex has been one of the Nos' few successes in the past few months and they have effectively managed to conflate the Yes campaign with a campaign about – as they would say – one man's ego. The No campaign has thrown everything in trying to caricature Alex as untrustworthy, aloof, arrogant and aggressive. This combined with their name calling and personal insults has of course had some effect.

Even after all of this Alex still remains by far the most popular leader of a political party, not just in Scotland, but throughout the UK, and the SNP remain incredibly popular even after seven years of Government. Leaders do become unpopular in the course of the leadership and Alex is just experiencing the normal rules of political gravity. Maybe we've not done enough to separate the Yes campaign from Alex, even though it is Nicola Sturgeon who has done so much of the heavy lifting for Yes. But the intervention from Jim Sillars is unhelpful and will only go to suggest problems in our leadership when we should be focusing on the real difficulties in theirs.

Sunday 18 May

A couple of opinion polls out today suggesting our progress in closing the gap has stalled if not reversed. An ICM poll showed the Nos have risen four percentage points to 46%, while Yes has fallen five points to 34%. The poll therefore gives the Nos a 12-point lead, up nine percentage points since last month but at the same level it had in a February survey by the same pollster. The second comes from our favourite pollster, Panelbase, which shows 47% would vote against independence – an increase of 2% with support for independence unchanged at 40%, with 13% undecided. The latter appears in the *Sunday Times* along with findings 'again' that English or non-Scottish-born residents are more likely to vote No. In a curious piece The *Times* seems to find it significant that English resident Scots might vote No and in a very sinister article even suggest this causing all sorts of issues and problems. Everybody, wherever they're from has the right to vote the way they want and I hope this 'ethnic' nonsense does not become a feature of the mainstream press coverage.

More importantly for the referendum there now seems to be clear evidence that our narrowing of the polls has stalled. There's two ways of looking at this. Firstly that it is a good thing. That we don't want to be leading in the polls just now so far out from the referendum date itself because a No lead leaves them in their complacency torpor and at ease to continue in their leadership fratricide. It also means that we won't be exposed to the increased scrutiny and antagonism that being in the lead brings. According to this argument we want to be neatly tucked in to pounce in the lead near the end of the campaign. The other argument is that this is where we actually are and that there is a genuine shift away from Yes as the economic consequences of the No arguments on currency and business are having an impact. I think we just have to sit tight and see where we are before the start of the Scottish summer holidays which are only a few short weeks away. Election day is quick approaching and this is getting very exciting.

Monday 19 May

This week is exclusively about the European elections, the last big test of the national mood before the independence referendum. We are all therefore totally focused on persuading as many people as possible to vote SNP instead of Yes this week. All expectations are that we will win the national share of the vote and every opinion poll has suggested that our win may actually be quite comfortable. Scotland has six Euro seats and other than the national percentages there's not much to play for. However, with the collapse of the Liberal vote their one seat is now up for grabs. A contest has therefore emerged for this last seat and it is shaping up between us securing a third seat or the seat going to UKIP. UKIP winning a Euro seat could be potentially disastrous for us in our emerging story that Scotland and the rest of the UK are on different political trajectories. So this week we will be upping the ante on UKIP in an attempt to depress their appeal and their vote.

It just so happens that it is Tasmina Ahmed-Sheikh who occupies our third place and no-one could better personify the new, modern Scotland with the Alf Garnett 1950s agenda of UKIP. All last week Tasmina was rounded on and spoke over by unionist men trying to stop her getting elected but in all these encounters she prevailed. Why this is important for the Yes campaign is highlighted in an opinion poll this morning that found that one in five Scots would be more likely to vote Yes in the referendum if UKIP wins large victories in the UK this week. I'm out and about all over Perthshire this week then ensuring that we get an SNP vote, but just as importantly depressing the UKIP vote.

Wednesday 21 May

Tense meeting in Scottish Parliament today where the leaders of both the Yes and No campaigns give evidence to the Parliament's Economy, Energy and Tourism committee. First up were the No campaign's director, Blair McDougall, and the under fire No leader, Alistair Darling. In a largely good-natured exchange with a committee with a majority of SNP MSPs the mood dramatically changed when Joan McAlpine asked Alistair Darling about meetings with his 'friend' the senior Treasury civil servant at the centre of ruling out a currency union, Sir Nicholas Macpherson.

On being asked this you could almost feel Darling squirm as he evaded answering, prompting Joan to say 'without full and frank disclosure, the inescapable conclusion is that he – as a backbench MP – has been directing policy announcements by the Treasury.' This was compounded when Blair McDougall conceded that he had been aware of the Treasury's advice about a currency union 'a matter of days before' it was made public. On this admission Darling did all he could to stop McDougall continuing in an almost comical attempt to 'shush' him. Dramatic stuff, which indeed suggests that the whole currency union refusal was directed by Darling and the No campaign. The Yes campaign has now demanded details of these meetings and will now move to try and determine what discussion did take place. Not counting on getting much information from a UK Treasury that is becoming the engine room of the No campaign.

Thursday 22 May

It's the European elections today and it is all about getting the vote out. In the usual Euro frustration we will be voting today but won't count till Sunday with the final result not coming till Monday because the Western Isles refuse to count on a Sunday. Trailing round the polling stations it's the usual slow response from the electorate though there is a sign that turnout is marginally up from five years ago. All signs are still showing us doing well and there is a good chance that we can secure that third seat. It is equally important that we keep

UKIP out and the press in Scotland have actually been playing their part in pointing out some of their more distasteful positions and quotes. The *Daily Record* in particular has a very powerful leader appealing to Scots not to vote for them. Out in the streets of Perth it's just enough to remind people the election is on. We should be the best organised in getting the vote out and our vote should also be the most motivated after months of indyref activity. Still a lot of people saying they're just not interested in Europe and therefore not voting. It's been a long day.

England also has council elections today and all eyes are on UKIP. It is the metropolitan councils and this usually tends to favour Labour. By 11pm results were coming in and it is clear that UKIP are doing well, taking seats from Labour as well as the Tories. Indeed an early result in the Labour stronghold in Rotherham shows big gains for UKIP. Heading off to bed Labour are ahead, but not by much, and UKIP are doing very well.

Friday 23 May

The results for the English councils are out and we political junkies are hooked to our news channels. Labour win the poll in England, but hardly convincingly, they top the poll with 31%, two points ahead of the Tories on 29%. UKIP came in on a credible 17% with the Liberals in meltdown. Where the UKIP result is very good it isn't extraordinary.

What this has done is to completely spook the UK parties who this morning are running around like headless chickens, perhaps appropriately, as Nigel Farage himself says that the result unleashes 'the UKIP fox in the Westminster chicken house'. Where we will need to see Sunday's result for any implications for the indyref this shows that the next UK election is all to play for. Labour's performance doesn't suggest an opposition ready to take power. English politics is totally fluid just now and these elections offer a tantalising glimpse for us in the Yes camp.

Sunday 25 May

I'm in the Bell's Sports Centre in Perth for the count and declaration for Perth and Kinross Council for the European elections. Election counts are curious affairs, and when it's not yours you can relax a little and even enjoy the bundles of ballot papers and the tension and excitement of our democracy in action. We're all there too. There are all the MSPs, councillors and lead activists and everyone actually enjoys our regular get togethers amidst all the ballot boxes. We're usually very good at our ballot box sampling but today our sampling goes a bit haywire and we give ourselves a bit of a scare.

In a lot of the council areas we see the Tories ahead and even in places where we are usually well ahead the Tory vote looks strong. This is important in constituencies where the Tories are the main challengers and where we watch them like hawks. The other thing we are looking out for is the UKIP vote. What we see is that they are polling strongly coming in anywhere between 10 to 12%. All round the hall there are anxious faces amongst the SNP camp and our poor sampling gives us only a marginal lead over the Tories. Even when the counting is complete we cannot declare before 10pm because there are still parts of Europe voting and somehow it is believed that the declaration of a result in Perth might have an impact on the good people of Palermo or Palma.

In the meantime we've been trying to get updates from colleagues across Scotland about what's happening in their local authorities' areas but any information is patchy. We are almost totally dependent on the official announcements and await these without any real intelligence. At a few minutes after ten we get our result and where it does show a swing towards the Tories it isn't as bad as we feared. Phew, says the candidate next in line for a decision by the Perthshire electors next year. We note our vote is slightly down, the Tories slightly up and UKIP at 10%, Labour is also up but their vote is so low in Perthshire that it is barely noticed. We then all head home to contact colleagues and watch the rest of the results come in.

Within the first few hours it is clear we are going to struggle to get that third MSP and UKIP look like they just might secure it. Where we have good results in the North East and Highlands we're still well behind in Glasgow and the Lanarkshires. At about 1am it becomes apparent that UKIP have secured that final seat. An obvious disappointment and something that will be much discussed tomorrow. We have won the popular vote and the election but it feels decidedly hollow with that UKIP gain. I had hoped that Scotland would reject them utterly and we now have to finesse our response to this pretty dramatic and unwelcome development.

Monday 26 May

As predicted UKIP have won the Euro election in the UK, quite convincingly, and Labour narrowly beat the Tories into third place. Only the votes from London stopped the official opposition coming behind a party of Government a year before a general election. In Scotland we have won the election with 29% of the poll with only a slight dip in our vote, Labour are up 4% at 25%, the Tories up a smidgeon on 17% with UKIP crucially fourth on just over 10%.

Already there is a battle of interpretation with all sides trying to win the narrative on what this means for the indyref. Some Nos seem to be almost celebrating UKIP's success as a mark against independence, but most are just trying to suggest that this upsets and even destroys our 'different countries' agenda. To get away with this they have to try and get round the fact that in the rest of the UK UKIP secured almost 30% where in Scotland it was still only 10%. There are also many unionists lumping all the votes for unionist parties together to again suggest that we have stalled. To make that work, some senior Better Together figures have included UKIP and even far right parties in the top up.

Looking at the rest of the UK, and even all over Europe, it is almost incredible that we as a party of Government won this election at all. We have been in Government for seven years but yet we still win elections. What we might be guilty of is raising expectations about our result with increasing talk of winning the third seat. This has been picked up as a 'failure' for the SNP. But it was the opinion polls that showed us in the mid-30s and reviewing our materials we only talked about winning this election and saw the third seat as a 'bonus'. We did shape the contest up between us and UKIP for that last seat, something that Labour are now trying to suggest tempted people into the UKIP camp, but that was entirely the right thing to do. We cannot ignore or pander to UKIP and we must take them on directly and give people a positive offer to vote for. The unionists also have the problem of managing the UKIP MEP, David Coburn. Should they offer him a place in 'Better Together' which he wants, or ignore him? In a chaotic interview on Good Morning Scotland he clearly will not be an asset to the No camp coming across as barely coherent.

Tuesday 27 May

For the past few days there has been growing 'excitement' about the release of the latest Treasury analysis paper about the costs of setting up an independent Scotland. This has been described as the most definitive analysis thus far and we are bracing ourselves for all the various portends of doom and gloom. Where this will be officially launched tomorrow there are various briefings and previews, and today, all the talk is about what's included. Because of this we are also hastily releasing our new paper on the financial benefits of independence as an obvious attempt to not give the Treasury a free hand and to try and spike their efforts.

The early reports from the Treasury talked of a figure of £2.7 billion to set up an independent Scotland but today this has been finessed downwards to £1.5 billion amidst all sort of claims of academics' works being misinterpreted and the almost unbelievable claim that an independent Scotland would need 180 new departments whilst the UK itself only has 42. This gets even more interesting in the evening when Professor Patrick Dunleavy from the LSE, who is credited with much of the Treasury's modelling, claiming that the Treasury's figures are 'bizarrely inaccurate' adding 'I don't see why the Scottish Government couldn't do this for a very small amount of money.' The front page of the *Financial Times* is then circulated on social media and it confirms that the academics at the heart of the Treasury's figures are disowning themselves entirely from the Treasury's interpretation of their figures. Absolute dynamite and sets up tomorrow as one of these very fascinating days in the independence referendum.

Wednesday 28 May

Just as we had the open goal of the nonsense over the Treasury figures any advantage has been compromised when we failed to give a figure on the costs of establishing an independent Scotland. Where John Swinney did a great job in dismantling the Treasury figures he was asked at least ten times and refused to give a figure on what the cost would actually be. Where this is almost an impossible figure to determine (we don't know what the result of negotiations with the UK will be) we should have at least been prepared for this question and ready with a convincing response.

This was gleefully picked up by Danny Alexander at the launch of the Treasury's report, almost disbelieving of the gift presented to him. He then got down to the familiar themes of independence being a costly and risky gamble before presenting the meat of his paper. He described the Treasury analysis as its most forensic document since the last Labour Government ruled out joining the Euro. Ignoring entirely the disputed figures he claimed that a Yes vote would see Scotland paying up to £1.5bn to build a new state, interest rates up to 1% higher, and new policy pledges that would cost £1.6bn a year. This would amount to a bill of £1,400 for each Scot. Only this wasn't a cost it was in fact a union dividend!

Half an hour earlier and almost within shouting distance, Alex Salmond, launched the hastily convened Scottish Government paper. In that we find that voting Yes would leave every person in Scotland £1,000 better off in 15 years' time, as the country profited from a booming economy and rising employment that would outstrip the

UK. This was described by the First Minister as an 'independence bonus' which would eventually be worth £5bn a year to the Scottish economy. He maintained that the gains would be secured without tax rises or spending cuts. Introducing the paper the FM said that 'People across Scotland will now be looking at the competing visions of our nation's future outlined today. Our vision, based on the extraordinary wealth of Scotland and the ability of the people who live here to run their own country, or that of a Tory-led Westminster Government intent on running Scotland down and whose bogus figures have been brutally exposed.'

In an interview with the BBC following the competing launches the First Minister attempted to steady the costs issue by offering a figure of £250 million, though with no real conviction and without any real evidence. He then went into a bit more detail about what immigrant numbers might be needed to come to Scotland to help deal with our demographic issues. An incredible day of claim and counterclaim with a phalanx of dodgy figures. Not sure what the public made of all of this but it's certainly been confusing, even for those of us charged with lobbing the grenades over the front line.

Thursday 29 May

'The politicised parading of sharply contrasting fiscal forecasts will win no prizes for objective economic assessment and risks alienating voters of both sides' concludes the *Financial Times*, and everywhere there is almost disbelief at both sets of figures. All over the press this is presented as a showdown and 'a war of words' have triggered 'bitter clashes' between Edinburgh and Westminster, with both sides accusing each other of producing 'bogus figures'. At 12pm we're off to the Scottish Parliament for First Minister's Questions, and where Johann Lamont leaves aside the figures battle both Ruth Davidson and Willie Rennie both ineptly try and make hay out of our difficulties. The problem for the unionists in pursuing this is that their figures are in just as bad shape as ours. What has developed, mostly due to our efforts, is a big pea-souper of a fog round all this with each side unable to properly lay into each other because of the overwhelming lack of clarity. Later in the day it seems that we have almost played this out and where we will face repeated calls to present our 'costs' it has more or less been fought to a standstill.

Three cinema chains, Vue, Odeon and Cineworld, along with Glasgow Film Theatre, have decided to withdraw pro-Union and pro-independence adverts claiming that cinemagoers wanted a 'retreat from the real world' when watching a film. This apparently follows complaints about some No ads. We invested quite a lot of effort in our ads so this does come as a disappointment but the Nos have really dragged them down particularly with a completely tasteless ad from the useless 'vote no borders' group which suggests that children from an independent Scotland wouldn't be able to use the facilities at the world-class St Ormond Street hospital, forcing even the hospital to clarify it was wrong and nothing to do with them. Little wonder that people booed that.

Friday 30 May

Independence costs again still dominate and today they are focused around comments made by a spokesperson for the First Minister admitting that Scots will not be told how much setting up an independent Scotland would cost ahead of September's referendum. It was one of our SpAds who made these remarks and I don't know who the description fits, but it certainly doesn't seem like Kevin Pringle. We seem to be digging ourselves further into trouble in this one and we need to find some way to get out of this. I don't know why we can't just give some ballpark figure and move on.

Today also signals the start of the regulatory period for the referendum. You can almost feel this long race beginning to edge into the closing furlongs and the finish line in sight. We're almost into June leaving three full months for campaigning and one of them, July, can be almost written off as most of Scotland's on holiday. This does not leave much time left at all. What the rules mean is that from today no individual or organisation can spend more than £10,000 on campaigning unless they are registered with the Commission as a permitted participant. Yes Scotland and Better Together, as designated lead campaigners, can spend a maximum of £1.5 million between now and the referendum, while political parties have their spending limits based on their share of the vote at the last Scottish Parliament election. Other registered campaigners can spend up to £150,000. That's a lot of money spinning around on this and from now on everything's for real.

June 2014

Tuesday 3 June

Not again! Apparently we have to endure another Labour No relaunch from Gordon Brown. He has now had more relaunches than a Soyuz spacecraft. Gushily serialised in the *Daily Record*, he also has a book to sell and I'm not sure where the gratuitous promotion of the book begins and his campaign for the union ends. It's all about our children, he says, and you can almost hear the violins in the background when he says 'This is about my children and my children's children. Anyone who is a parent who is entering this campaign knows that this is not similar to a general election vote or similar to an ordinary vote in a council election or a European election.' Not saying anything new other than a bizarre plan to establish a 'senate-style' upper chamber to replace the House of Lords should Scotland vote No in September! Word coming back from Brown's meetings is that he drones on in that caged tiger prowling thing he does before the audience are curtly told that there will be no questions, but punters are being offered the opportunity to buy one of his books and have it signed.

Wednesday 4 June

Queen's speech today and it's hats and tails and Government lite as the zombie Parliament unveils its final programme. Most of us MPs who can't be bothered with the pomp and ceremony turn up to the Commons not to see Black Rod summon us to the House of donors and cronies but to hear the 'Beast's Speech', the now traditional quip offered by the Beast of Bolsover, Dennis Skinner, which is now as traditional as anything Her Majesty pronounces. This year with almost perfect timing Dennis shouts out 'coalition's last stand' as Black Rod turns round to head back to the Lords. The speech itself offered nothing but we did learn that Her Majesty's Government would 'work to keep Scotland in the UK'. That's alright then.

In the afternoon the first editions of an extraordinary interview with Alistair Darling in the *New Statesman* emerge. In an almost mad series of incoherent ramblings Alistair Darling compares Alex Salmond to North Korea's Kim Jong-IL. Seemingly this was deemed fair enough because of Alex's reasonable assessment that Scotland returned a UKIP MEP because of the many BBC UKIP images 'beamed' into Scottish living rooms as part of their non-stop coverage of every move of the UKIP leader. How this equation could be made only exists in the recesses of Alistair Darling's head. Worse though was Darling's claim that our peaceful, inclusive democratic, civil, independence movement was 'blood and soil' ethnic nationalism. I at first did not quite understand the significance of this assessment until people started circulating the Wikipedia entry on what 'blood and soil' actually meant. Only then did we all learn the full horror of what we in the SNP were engaged in. *'Blut und Boden'* to give it its proper German translation was the term the Nazis used to support their 'ethnic' nationalism, It literally means the blood of the people and the claim of the territory. Yessers quite rightly became furious and all sorts of calls for an apology and retraction emerged everywhere.

In the evening the Nos were in full retreat claiming the Kim Jong-IL quip 'was a joke' – this from an Alistair Darling not exactly renowned for his sense of humour. No supremo, Blair McDougall then revealed that a clarification from the *New Statesman* would soon be released on *'Blut and Boden'*. Not long after the *New Statesman* put up a revised piece with a clarification and a transcript. In the transcript instead of any Darling comment on 'blood and soil, we had 'inaudible mumble'! Apparently the reach of the Nos extends to what is and what was said in an interview. It was also totally craven of the *New Statesmen* to allow itself to be bullied in this way from the No campaign. It is also the case that the Nos had been circulating the earlier copy with the 'blood and soil' reference and only when they saw the true significance of that remark did they seek to 'clarify' it.

In the evening I won an award for my social media output from PICTFOR, or the 'Parliamentary Internet Communications and

Technology Forum' to give it its full name. I am the most mentioned MP on Twitter! Where it doesn't rank with the Oscars or the BRITS I'm actually quite proud of this little award. Twitter is where so much of the debate is just now and where news is made and debate engaged. It came as a total surprise to me that I have beaten so many big political names, so where I'm all self-deprecating in public, I'm actually quite chuffed. I've even been asked on *Daily Politics* tomorrow to talk about it.

Thursday 5 June

First thing this morning I was interviewed by three of the young people from the impressive BBC project 'Generation 2014'. These are undecided 16–18-year-olds and their series of interviews and presentations are being featured on the BBC News channel and Radio 1. Three very nice and engaged young people quizzed me on everything from Europe to tuition fees to the role of MPs. They conceded to me in private that, where they are still undecided, though they were veering towards Yes. This is good news as we are still having difficulties with the under-18s. After me they were away to interview Danny Alexander at the Treasury. Sure his grand office will be a bit more posh than the Portcullis House canteen where I saw them.

Because Scots obviously have great difficulty in understanding some of the nuances in the indyref debate the Nos deployed a Lego army to explain what Scots could buy with the £1,400 union dividend they claim we secure from the UK. In what must be just about the most tawdry and patronising intervention so far the Treasury and Scotland Office jointly published pictures of Lego figures demonstrating this largesse on BuzzFeed.

The Scots were informed that it could have a fish supper every day for about ten weeks, or we could 'scoff' 280 hotdogs at the Edinburgh Festival, while washing it down with lashings of Bovril watching Aberdeen get beat at football. It ends up saying we could all celebrate 'with endless hugs from everyone to celebrate still being part of the United Kingdom'. When it first appeared, I like most others thought it was a spoof put up by one of our Yes-supporting websites. But no, this was real and almost unbelievable. After hours of ridicule the Nos did the 'lacking sense of humour' stuff, apparently, we just didn't get it.

A bit more serious was Barack Obama's comments on independence at a joint press conference in Brussels with David Cameron at a G7 meeting. In what was a surprising and dramatic intervention Obama said the UK was 'one of the closest allies that we will ever have' adding it was a 'strong, robust, united and effective partner' saying the 'United Kingdom has been an extraordinary partner to us.' From the outside at least, it looks like things have worked pretty well. Though he stressed: 'but ultimately these are decisions that are going to be made by the folks there.'

You could almost immediately hear the cheers all the way from No towers and they immediately went into overdrive. In what were quite good interventions, for them, we even had the amusing 'audacity of nope'. They then got down to the business of changing their leaflet for their evening canvassing.

Though hardly unequivocal this was one of the interventions we didn't want. Obama is such a respected and important figure in Scotland and his comments will carry a lot of weight. Alex immediately went on TV to say to the President that with independence the US would have two friends and allies rather than one and using one of Obama's own phrases to respond to the comments, saying 'Yes we can'. I'm pretty sure that there are few people in Scotland waiting for the President of the United States comments to decide how they will vote in the independence campaign and it will make very little difference to the undecideds. What it does do is to add to the context of supporters and today the Nos secured a pretty impressive scalp.

Friday 6 June

Fringe comics are 'too afraid of abuse' to tell jokes about the Scottish referendum. This is once again down to the 'bitter tone of the debate' and cybernats have been blamed for the reluctance to make fun of the nation's big political event. *The Scotsman* reports that 'two out of the four major Fringe venues have nothing at all in their programme related to the debate'. While another two venues have only one show each on a referendum theme. Online warriors have ensured that 'venues and performers have been put off by the level of abuse meted out to comedians such as Susan Calman, Eddie Izzard and Rory Bremner, and even Yes playwright Alan Bissett'. The thing is you would have to have a heart of stone not to find humour everywhere in the debate about independence and some of it has been quite hilarious. If anything the indyref is made for satire and I'm sure we could all do with a laugh about what's going on.

What is rib-ticklingly hilarious is the request from Lego to have their products removed from the terrible No campaign, £1,400 nonsense. Lego UK said it had not granted permission for the images to be used and that they were used without the company's knowledge. They said 'We have requested that the images are removed due to our neutral political stance. We are a children's toy company and therefore all of our communication is targeted towards children'. The Nos shouldn't be too disappointed though, there's always play-dough and plasticine.

Sunday 8 June

Tomorrow it will be one hundred days to the indyref. At the start of the campaign it was said it would be too long, that people would lose interest and that the campaigns wouldn't be sustained. Quite the opposite. It has gone in really quickly and has energised the whole of Scotland. Sometimes, if you were to believe some of our unionist friends, you would think that we are currently living in some sort of dreadful conflict zone. A fearful, intimidating place, inhabited by 'vile cybernats' waiting for the next Twitter post to crush the 'yoon' enemy with their insults, barbed comments and parody sites. It's a world where multi-millionaire business leaders cower behind their B&Q shelters as they remain ever fearful of the 'Salmond hordes' that roam the land keeping them from speaking out in support of their treasured union.

The truth is that no nation has indulged in a debate about its future as maturely and respectfully as Scotland has, and this is to our immense credit. It is a debate that has gripped and energised the nation, reinvigorated town hall politics with the possible participation of some 80% of our population in the vote itself. No-one has even suffered from a bloodied nose in the cause of Scottish independence and the police aren't being called out to see down arguments far less street demonstrations or violent confrontations. When there have been issues they have been so unusual that they have been a story because of their peculiarity!

Because the Nos can't find any real 'dark' side to our civic independence movement they've focussed on the idea of the 'cybernat'. They use this recent invention as a means to build the picture of an intolerant, abusive 'nationalist' who inhabits some sort of twilight zone waiting to pounce, bully and silence the innocent, honest voice of the Nos.

Where there are of course some dreadful Yes online contributors, whose interventions are awful, abusive and totally counterproductive the 'cybernat' has almost become an online folk demon with a reputation as fearful as it is exaggerated. The creation of the 'cybernat' also serves a much more sinister purpose and that is to silence criticism of the unionist case. We have next to no support from the mainstream media and the arrival of citizen journalism and the many Yes-supporting websites has immeasurably helped promote the Yes case. Many of these new commentators are not the polished voices of the MSM and any indiscretion means they are immediately punished and conveniently lumped in the category labelled 'cybernat' in an attempt to diminish and undermine their contribution.

But for all their efforts this just passes the public by, and they remain bemused by an inconsequential online skirmish that is so far removed from their everyday experience of how the debate is actually being conducted. This is why our debate is so remarkable. Even with all the attempts to try and talk the debate down and create these online bogeymen the debate about our future remains one of the most positive, exciting and engaging debates that we have ever conducted as a nation. Instead of denigrating this incredible exercise we should all be celebrating it.

Monday 9 June

The Nos main job today is to reveal their new identity and slogan, and it seems that at last the Nos are embracing their No-ness. Ingeniously titled 'No thanks' we are told that where Better Together will still be the campaign name it will be 'No thanks' that will adorn most of their material.

The No thing has been troubling them for a while. Having their case as the negative or rejection is not a particularly comfortable place to be when positivity is required to win. They have spent a lot of time running away from the reality of the ballot paper 'No' that awaits them. Time is running out, and they had to come up with something that captures their campaign with the option of a No vote. I think they have almost achieved that today and things like 'independence, no thanks', is almost a positive rejection. We'll wait to see what the public think.

A rare treat for me today as I secured an invitation to the press gallery lunch in the House of Commons to hear, who else but Gordon Brown. On my way up I met the BBC's James Landale who is the current chair of the press gallery who informed me that Brown would actually be taking questions! James reminded me that they could only come from the journalists present.

I, predictably, was the only 'Nat' in the Westminster village and I was given a lot of 'what on earth is he doing here' looks with Brown himself grudgingly acknowledging my presence. That didn't stop him letting loose. In a remarkable ramble I could hardly believe what I was hearing as he criticised the No campaign for being negative, particularly about the currency. He also said that Cameron should debate Salmond and that the whole 'Better Together' campaign was almost fighting the wrong battles. Brown and Darling famously don't get on, and he had real difficulty in even mentioning Darling's name. Brown is a very complicated and divisive figure and all of this is certainly not going to endear him to his No friends. The Nos want Brown on board because they believe in the Brown popularity in Scotland stuff. Got a sense his phone will be red hot when he gets into the lift for the long trip down from the Westminster press Moncrieffe's restaurant.

Tuesday 9 June

The *New Statesman*, with that full Darling interview, is out today and the *New Statesman* have released the recording with Darling's response to those 'blood and soil' comments. There have now been two corrections to the various pieces but today is about clearing it all up. What Darling does say, or agreed to when put to him, is that we are 'at heart' blood and soil nationalists. I suppose that's alright then...

The association of the SNP and the wider Yes movement with nazism is something that exists at the fringes of the No campaign and is taken up enthusiastically by the Labour blogger, Ian Smart. But inferring that the 47% of Scottish voters are in some way nazi or support nazi parties is just absurd and insulting to the intelligence of the Scottish people. The people of Scotland know that we are an inclusive, peaceful and civic movement so I have no idea why the Nos think it's a good thing to dwell on this stuff. It probably hurts them more than it does us.

I was also speaking in the Queen's Speech today and was surprised I was taken early in a debate without time limits. I used my speech to pick up on the 'Scotland Bit' in the Queen's Speech where Her Majesty said 'My Government will continue to put the case for Scotland' remaining within the UK. I love making speeches in the House of Commons and will so miss it when there will be no further opportunities.

Wednesday 10th June

The Nos held a pretty effective rally on Monday in their 100-day pitch to female voters and those Labour supporters tempted to vote Yes. One of their key speakers was the self-styled 'ordinary mum' Claire Lally. Her speech was heartfelt and, for a No, pretty convincing. The only thing is, where she may indeed be an ordinary mum she is also an ordinary member of Labour's shadow cabinet. This was something that the First Minister's senior Special Advisor, the impeccably nice guy, Campbell Gunn, felt obliged to advise a *Daily Telegraph* journalist in a private email. But not only did Campbell feel it necessary to reveal her Labour membership he also felt it was important to reveal that she was related to former Glasgow Labour provost, Pat Lally, (she isn't). This has now just about gone off the indyref-Richter scale this morning.

This is being characterised as a 'disgusting' smear. Labour are saying that 'For a taxpayer-funded advisor to attack the mother of a disabled child (yes she is a carer and mother of a disabled child) for giving an opinion about the referendum is a new low for the nationalists'. This is therefore all the proof that they need to contend that the cybernat smear campaigns are being coordinated by Alex Salmond's office.

They then almost cheerily posted all the abuse that Claire Lally received following these revelations from some of the online recalcitrants whom you could always rely on to help the Nos make the 'evil cybernat' case. We, or the FM's office, were also doubly guilty for 'unleashing' all this abuse at this poor woman. As the story progressed all sorts of calls for Campbell to resign or be sacked appeared with the view that he broke the ministerial code (he didn't). Later in the afternoon Campbell apologised unreservedly and was backed by the First Minister.

In all an episode that couldn't have been more fabricated in its outrage. Campbell certainly got it wrong in the connection with Pat Lally and it was right that he apologised. But his main crime in the view of the No parties was that he was trying to smear Claire Lally for mentioning her Labour connections to a journalist. It is just a bizarre and almost silly allegation but it is taken seriously because of this demand to find all sorts of evidence of foul play and something dark at the heart of the Yes/independence operation. This case was given legs with the response from some so-called Yes supporters online.

Just as we were getting to grips with the Claire Lally episode another huge story was breaking. JK Rowling has just announced she is backing No and was giving Better Together a million pounds. In a cogent and well-drafted personal statement she described why she was voting No and, other than some nonsense about bloodlines and ethnicity, it was a convincing case for a No vote. She said 'My hesitance at embracing independence has nothing to do with lack of belief in Scotland's remarkable people or its achievements. The simple truth is Scotland is subject to the same 21st-century pressures as the rest of the world'. And 'The more I listen to the Yes campaign, the more I worry about its minimisation and even denial of risks.'

No real surprise that she is backing No as she has been to Better Together events and is a known personal friend of the Browns. In her statement she cutely said she had looked seriously at Yes before opting for staying together. Fair enough, and good on her. It was then what followed that became the story. JK Rowling was immediately subject to a torrent of abuse online and it went on all day. Securing this was probably more valuable to the Nos than the money. In one day they have been able to present the whole Yes campaign as a bunch of misogynist bullies who throw vile abuse around on everybody from ordinary mums to worldwide celebrities.

As we were retiring to bed news was emerging of an opinion poll which was 'very good' for Yes. Unfortunately we couldn't tempt David Clegg, the *Record*'s political editor to tell us more.

Thursday 11 June

Thirty-nine per cent plan to vote Yes with 44% saying No. If you remove those who have still to make up their mind that would give a wafer-thin majority to No with a result of 53% No and 47% Yes. That is the news in the *Daily Record* this morning. Even more encouragingly it found that we will win the referendum if voters believe that the Tories will win the next election. Under that scenario 54% said they would vote Yes and 46% No. This is a great poll for us and is most welcome after what had seemed like a stalling or even reversal of our early spring momentum. The findings about the Tories are most useful as Labour are looking anything like dead certs to win the next UK election just now and so few people believe that the awkward Ed Miliband will ever be Prime Minister. We now have to ramp up the democratic deficit arguments and keep our focus on the Tories. Great stuff.

Almost totally predictably all three opposition leaders raise the issue of Campbell Gunn at FMQ's. Probably even more predictably they called for him to resign or be sacked. The FM made a fantastic response to them saying Campbell had made a mistake and a misjudgement. All sorts of various things were thrown into their question in their attempt to conflate Campbell's private email to cybernat attacks on JK Rowling and their contention that the SNP are nothing but appalling bullies that co-ordinate all this dreadful activity. In response Alex said that 'All of us, every single one of us, should condemn abuse on the internet... Every single one of us should condemn that handful of mindless idiots who engage in such things in the early hours of the morning.'

He added: 'We should as a Parliament and as a society stand up against that handful of people who are attempting to pollute this independence debate.' Exactly, and I hope that all of those who engage in these personal attacks are listening and perhaps think about the damage they are doing to our cause.

The UK Government have also announced that they will spend £720,000 on a booklet outlining the benefits of staying in the UK to be sent to each house in the UK. The Scotland Office has produced more than 2.5 million of these 16-page leaflets with all the nonsense from the Scotland Analysis series of 14 papers with their take on independence. After all the stuff we get about the cost of the White Paper this is almost breathtaking. At least we have a mandate to bring forward a referendum. This will now mean that they can no longer drone on about the costs of Scottish Government publications so almost grateful for this latest intervention.

Saturday 14 June

Oh no! The Holy Father is apparently backing the union. Well sort of. What he in fact did say is that he was worried about 'divisions' when interviewed by a Spanish newspaper. In more of a philosophical intervention he looked at the example of Yugoslavia where he concluded that 'there are nations with cultures so different that couldn't even be stuck together with glue'. Then he considered whether that was perhaps the case in Scotland, The Nos are all over this and are naturally delighted. Some of course have wondered where it leaves the No coalition as the Orange Order is just about the most strident of the No voices.

Sunday 15 June

Another fantastic opinion poll in the *Sunday Herald* this morning. A Panelbase survey has found a record 43% for Yes with 47% for No, leaving it 52–48 when the don't knows are stripped out. This is very encouraging and just what is required. There has been a real sense of a stalling recently and even some of the conversation we are finding on the doorstep has suggested a drifting away since the spring. The Unionists predictably point to the fact that this poll was commissioned by us and is in the Yes-supporting *Sunday Herald*. But it is a fully weighted survey by a reputable pollster and is the same as all other opinion polls. If we can just stay within a few points and continue to present this as neck and neck we can still hope for big mistakes from the Nos whilst doing the conversion work quietly behind the scenes. This poll very much helps that important work and has been a big boost this morning.

Meanwhile over at the *Scotland on Sunday* we have another poll and it is equally encouraging, only they are being a little bit more coy in announcing this 'good news'. They have found support for independence up two points to 36% whilst No has fallen three points to 43%. When undecided voters were excluded the support for independence stood at 45%, an increase of three percentage points on last month. This has obviously been perceived as too much of a good news story for the Yes side that the *Scotland on Sunday* has instead majored on other findings in the poll such as divisions and post-referendum rancour. We are therefore left with stuff about families 'divided' and friendships tested.

Monday 16 June

Spent the day filming a piece for the new BBC Scotland referendum programme, Scotland 2014. I have been a constant critic of the new programme and for such I have been rewarded with a ten-minute op-ed piece on 'Britishness' and 'nationalism'! I was given control of the script and asked to identify three people who I could interview and chose Professor James Mitchell, one of Scotland's pre-eminent authorities on social attitudes, former MSP and columnist, Andrew Wilson, who first delved into the issue of Britishness to much controversy and disapproval about 15 years ago and blogger Kate Higgins who hosted my first piece on the issue on her blog. Was a fantastic day and got some really interesting shots in the city centre of a very sunny Edinburgh.

Also in the city, ironically, at Edinburgh's folly on Calton Hill, our friends in the Better Together campaign were issuing their joint statement on more powers. Unable to secure an agreed position on 'more powers' they needed to show there was some agreement between them and this was about the best they could do. They were all there, with the slogan 'more powers, guaranteed' they now believe that they are able to offer at least some sort of joint position on this.

Wednesday 18 June

In the latest instalment of the never-ending franchise of the evil cybernats, Wings Over Scotland, has been disowned by the Yes campaign; or rather it has instructed a local group to stop distributing material endorsing the Wings Over Scotland website. This follows a complaint by Conservative MSP Alex Johnstone, who was described by Wings Over Scotland as a 'fat troughing scum' for his campaign of harassing the lottery winners, the Weirs, for donating millions of pounds to Yes. This is a contribution typical of Wings and his increasingly foul-mouthed and provocative outpourings have become increasingly embarrassing to the Yes campaign.

Wings is a peculiar feature amongst the new independence-supporting websites. It is particularly well written and does a forensic job in debunking some of the more fanciful unionist press stories. Its main contribution is the Wee Blue Book which has become particularly popular with Yes activists and it is now a regular feature in Yes stalls up and down the country. What the White Paper does in over a hundred thousand words the WBB does in a concise 74-page pocket-size journal. It puts the economic case for independence in an appealing easily understood way and even those of us who are uncomfortable about the increasingly unhelpful Wings' outbursts regularly turn to it when we need a quick answer.

Fronted by the self-styled 'Reverend' Stuart Campbell, a former Liberal and games journalist it is run from his home in Bath. The press particularly loathe Wings, and the website has featured heavily in the 'vile cybernat' exposes. The 'Reverend' perhaps doesn't help his cause much with his curious comments on such things as 9/11 and Hillsborough. However, proscribing Wings isn't going to go down well amongst the wider Yes support and it does suggest a backing down in the face of unionist press pressure. Pretty sure that Wings will remain unperturbed by this 'ban' and the Reverend will continue to do his job and I'm also pretty sure we'll all still be reading it.

It was Rock the Boat tonight, the second part of MP4's ten-year anniversary organised by the UK Music Industry the BPI. For most of our ten years the BPI have hired us a boat moored at Westminster pier so MPs can make the short walk to the boat then provide them with free drink and a barbecue. Tonight was a fantastic night and the BPI gave us all a gold disk to recognise our ten years and £1 million raised for charity. Great night.

Thursday 19 June

Today Danny Alexander was signing off the Government's booklet dubbed 'Project Fact' which is to be mailed to every home in Scotland. It is apparently the case for 'opposition to independence' itself designed to 'demolish nationalist fiction'. This is the booklet the UK Government are spending almost ¾ of a million on and it is being sent out without barely a question from the media.

Friday 20 June

The *Record* front page leads with 'Wanted' highlighting the news that 'a number of vacancies have recently become available for talented bean-counters to calculate the cost of setting up an independent country'. Independence start-up costs have just about become the Nos' favourite campaign theme just now and they believe that they are on to something. Start-up costs are going to be almost impossible to determine because we just don't know how helpful the UK Government are going to be following independence. They will be dependent on negotiations and of course the UK Government are not going to prenegotiate so then we go round again and again. Alex has hinted at figures and if the Nos want a figure without being prepared to help negotiate one then we should just give a figure and stick with it. It would save all this nonsense and waste of time.

In a referendum debate at Blairgowrie High School this afternoon and, boy, is it hard work. I went up early to hear the debating society debate the issue and was surprised how quickly the clichés of the referendum discourse were so easily traded, almost effortlessly. All the usual themes were there and the whole debate could have been interchanged with any debate amongst any age group anywhere in the country. The debate references are now so ingrained that they seem almost unmovable. Later in front of the whole upper school

I debate with the Tory group leader on Perth and Kinross Council, Mac Roberts. I really put it out there and I had the whole school listening intently believing that I was being totally convincing and persuasive. This was made easier by my No opponent being almost embarrassing and barely coherent. Believing that I had done a great job they took a vote and we were absolutely hammered securing only about 28% of the vote. I know that we have had trouble in some of these school debates but this was almost calamitous. I hope that this is just peculiar to Blairgowrie but it is very concerning.

Sunday 22 June

Looks like we are going to have a referendum debate after all following a grudging acceptance by the First Minister to a debate with Alistair Darling. In accepting the debate Alex continues to urge Cameron to debate with him saying he would be prepared to accept Darling or another No campaign nominee as a substitute. The press are trying to suggest that Alex has 'blinked first' and are claiming this as a victory for the Nos even though we have always said that he would debate. This is going to be tough for Darling. He just does not possess the range of skills to get him through a debate with someone as proficient as Alex. He is also increasingly flaky and unpredictable (his recent blood and soil nonsense) and he can't seem to stop himself from becoming angry and flustered even in easy interviews, not a good look for a watching public. He also hasn't exactly been given the most enthusiastic of backing from No high command, particularly the Tory side of it. If I was the Nos I'd seriously be thinking about putting someone like Douglas Alexander up, someone who can talk calmly and persuasively. The Nos certainly should be doing everything to keep Darling away from the debating lectern.

Tuesday 24 June

Our friends in the House of Lords are debating independence again and they're tripping over each other to attend and speak out. Apparently 40 Lords have requested to speak and listening to them they can barely help themselves from sounding other worldly, patronising and ill-informed. We have increasingly turned the House of Lords into an independence issue and there is anger that an unelected institution can lecture the Scots on our democratic future. We have therefore described them as 'an affront to democracy' a 'bloated chamber' stuffed full of 'cronies, donors and party placemen'. The Lords then has almost become the personification of the 'Westminster establishment' and because of its inherent ridiculousness it has become an easy and convenient target. They have brought themselves into the fray with debates such as this and therefore deserve every bit of scorn they get.

Oh no! Just we all thought we had secured the debate it looks like it might be off. Apparently the fall out is all about timing. STV said that the proposed date of 15 July was non-negotiable only for the First Minister's office to remind them that the First Minister would only debate the Prime Minister before the opening of the Commonwealth Games. STV then decided to change the date till August only for 'Better Together' angrily pulling out alleging that STV were willing to change the date at the request of the First Minister. Better Together have then gone off on one about STV backing down to pressure and they are just looking silly. Don't know if this will happen or not but meanwhile over on the BBC it looks like there will be a televised debate on 12 August. There will be a debate and Better Together should grow up a little about how it will happen

Saturday 28 June

Today Stirling hosts both the Bannockburn 800 event and the UK's Armed Forces Day. I don't think anyone doubts that the UK Government chose to hold this event in Stirling today to set it up against Bannockburn and try and spike the emotional impact of the Bannockburn event. The unionists really have a thing about Bannockburn and have been almost compulsively anxious about the iconography of the Bannockburn centenary. They put Armed Forces Day up against the event in the hope that there would be an outpouring of UK solidarity, particularly with all the First World War commemorations.

The thing is very few people care and practically no-one is giving it a second thought. However, that hasn't diminished the almost paranoia of the UK Government who have even sent the Prime Minister northwards again. The result is we have a congested Stirling struggling to accommodate everyone who wants to attend either of the pretty tedious events.

Sunday 29 June

Day two of the 'Battle of Stirling' and it's all about the black ops this morning. Apparently our Prime Minister has been spreading pro-Union propaganda. During the celebrations held in Stirling! Cameron said the UK military kept 'Scots safe' and urged them to vote No whilst Better Together campaign material was distributed to military personnel alongside a reminder about registering to vote. The *Sunday Herald* even has a leaked email showing that the Cabinet Office asked the Ministry of Defence in April to 'cascade' pro-Union material through the ranks of the armed forces using email.

All of this is so unnecessary as the Nos must know they already have the bulk of the armed forces' vote. Anyone who marches under the Union Jack and gets involved in UK military adventures are almost certainly going to have a greater sense of UK unity. This weekend just confirms the view that most of the energy they have wasted on this has been a supreme waste of time and effort. We didn't come out to play, instead we congratulated both events and just let the unionists get on with it.

There's a second demonstration at the BBC headquarters today and this time it looks quite big. Where there is always a dispute about numbers at these demos there looks like well over a thousand people there. Patience is certainly being stretched to breaking point by the BBC and their institutional bias for a No vote is now apparent to anyone with even a passing interest in the debate.

Questions are always stacked in favour of the Nos and nearly every headline is of a 'warning' or a 'blow' to the SNP and Yes camp. There is also the very useful work done by the West of Scotland University which showed the No side gets the bulk of the BBC Scotland news coverage. Let's also not forget the totally one-sided nature of the BBC UK coverage with its endless procession of commentators totally committed to a No vote.

But this demonstration just looks bad and it is all too easy for the Nos to present this as Yes paranoia and an attempt to bully the BBC. On the other hand, the Beeb being the centre of this sort of protest is quite sensitive to allegations of bias. I think there will be any number of meetings in Pacific Quay to see what they can do to try and dampen this down in case it gets out of hand. Incredible that so many people have turned up and care enough about how the referendum is covered. Would much prefer they were out canvassing for Yes instead.

Monday 30 June

Cameron's making a statement in the House after failing to stop Jean-Claude Juncker becoming head of the EU Commission. Cameron called for a vote at the EU council and lost the vote 26 to 2, with only Hungary supporting the UK position. I ask him if this means that UK are even closer to the exit door and the only way for Scotland to retain its EU membership is to vote Yes in September? It was no great surprise that he did not agree with me. The UK's isolation and failure to enlist support in Europe does mean that the Euro-sceptics in the Tory ranks will be emboldened – we saw that in their response to the statement today – it also means that the proposed EU referendum will be fought over the UK's current arrangements. We now have to ramp up the suggestion that the only way to retain our membership is to vote Yes and continue to say that the UK is practically halfway out the exit to isolation.

July 2014

Thursday 3 July

Got a note late last night to tell me that the Prime Minister would be visiting my constituency, with the usual instruction not to share this information or publicise it – as if I would! Cameron's coming to address the Conservative Friends of the Union in the Dewar's Centre in Perth and as usual it is a closed meeting to an invited audience. He's making a pitch to the 'silent majority' to come forward and speak out, only of course, the silent majority of non-Tory voters will be kept out by the PM's security spooks.

Friday 4 July

The main purpose of Cameron's visit is the launch of the aircraft carrier the HMS *Queen Elizabeth*, an absolute behemoth of an industrial warship. Longer than three football pitches it is the biggest warship ever built by the UK. The Queen was at Rosyth to officially name it by smashing a bottle of Islay malt whisky onto the hull. Built at six locations around the UK it is the first of two aircraft carriers under construction. Famously bereft of aircraft, this and the second carrier, named the Prince of Wales, will be built at Rosyth regardless of the outcome of the referendum. That didn't stop all sort of indyref discourse whether through the symbolism or direct confrontation.

Cameron told us 'If the United Kingdom stays together, as I hope it will, Glasgow and Scotland will continue to be an absolute centre of excellence in terms of shipbuilding. Let's celebrate today the fact that so many people have worked so hard to produce the Royal Navy's biggest ever ship. It's a really exciting day for Scotland, a great day for the United Kingdom and a sign of things to come if our country stays together.' This signalled the usual predictions that shipbuilding would cease in Scotland and the usual stuff that the UK doesn't build complex warships outside the UK, even though it does.

The First Minister carefully avoids all this in his address and instead talks of the skills of the workforce saying, 'What keeps us safe for the future is not the willpower of David Cameron, it's this magnificent deep water facility and the great skills of the workforce.' He even took along his dad, a veteran who served in the Navy during the war. My dad worked at Rosyth dockyard when it dominated the economy of West Fife in the '60s and '70s employing tens of thousands of people. Practically every family in the Dunfermline area had somebody who worked in the dockyard. Such was its role in the local economy that at school we even sat the 'dockyard exam' to place us at the level we would start our dockyard career. In those days we were told that devolution would destroy employment at Rosyth, now of course it is independence. Only a few thousand souls now work at the dockyard and it a mere shadow of its former self. The UK Government will continue to suggest that what is left of this activity will go with independence and I have no doubt that people will still believe them – even when the historic evidence stares them in the face.

Monday 7 July

The bullying theme goes through the roof today with the broadcast of a Channel 4 *Dispatches* programme with 'evidence' on how the SNP and the Yes campaign are intimidating businesses and organisations.

First in the frame is that appalling bully, Angus Robertson, my Westminster colleague, who represents most of Scotland's whisky distilleries. This 'thug' had the audacity to 'meet' the boss of the Scotch Whisky Association, Gavin Hewitt on six occasions, where the poor Mr Hewitt apparently 'felt' that there was a genuine fear that by coming out publicly against independence, there would be 'retribution down the track'. He even 'thought' that he (Angus) was trying 'to neuter business comment'.

If that wasn't conclusive enough next up was that 'Flashman' of Scottish politics the great oppressor, John Swinney, who even went as far as to 'pressure' Government and public organisations to pull out of the CBI after it backed a No vote. 'Unbelievably' he contacted bodies like VisitScotland and Skills Development Scotland, suggesting it 'may' be inappropriate to remain (as a public body) in an organisation that had hoisted its mast as a No campaigning organisation. What absolutely dreadful behaviour from this, thankfully, now exposed tyrant.

Even though this 'evidence' could only be regarded by any reasonable person as being on the 'thin' side the Nos went to town. All of this 'won't come as a surprise to those who've found themselves on the wrong end of an SNP tirade' said one, 'the Scottish Government using its position to breathe down the neck of everyone who dares disagree is frankly appalling' said another.

Almost unbelievably this was kicked around all day and otherwise sane journalists took it seriously. In watching the programme it was almost apologetic in the poverty of its 'evidence' and even the rehashed 'silencing the academics' seemed almost comical. Dreadful stuff from Channel 4 and does nothing for the quality of the debate.

Meanwhile on the BBC, Robert Peston managed to show how it could be done. In a very informative half hour he's almost even-handed in looking at the financial issues of independence. The broadcasters have to try and up their game and get this together. The unhappiness with the BBC in particular is becoming a real issue in the referendum and the charge of institutional bias in our national broadcasters is becoming almost a story in itself.

Wednesday 9 July

Doctor Who is probably the most mentioned TV programme in the indyref and it's back today. The first episode of the latest series of *Doctor Who*, which features Glaswegian actor Peter Capaldi in his first full appearance in the role, has what is described as a 'cheeky swipe' at independence. The script for the episode, which was leaked online, has a joke about the Dr saying his eyebrows might be declaring independence. In a rare glimpse of humour, albeit poor humour, from a Better Together spokesman we get 'Alex Salmond will be furious. He'll be sending his Daleks round to Ecks-terminate Peter Capaldi.' I'm holding my sides.

Thursday 10 July

Thought I was going to get back early to Scotland today but I got a late bid to appear on *Daily Politics* to talk about our national football side. A Tory MP Laurence Robertson has submitted an early day motion calling for a unified national UK team and it has been met with the usual howls of disapproval. This seems to come around before practically every international sporting event and I had a Commons debate on this when the previous Labour Government tried to dragoon a reluctant Scotland into a team GB in advance of the London Olympics. In a good-natured exchange I put the Tory in his place and managed to put in a few good indyref points. This is really good for us and we have got to try and ramp this up and get Yes as the natural repository for Scottish football fans. Again though, I already detected that our press team does not share my enthusiasm to pursue this at all.

Question Time was from Inverness tonight and uniquely there were no politicians on the panel. In what was a bizarre programme we were introduced to Nigel Kirk-Hanlin who gave an incredible contribution from the floor. Practically bursting with passion and unrestrained excitement he promised to even 'give his life' to save the union even invoking Jesus and voicing an incoherent rallying war cry. I think the Nos have just found their first hero of their campaign.

Friday 11 July

Our response to the emergency data retention emergency legislation was ramped up today. I got a call from Nicola Sturgeon who told me that she was anticipating this as a question in a debate she was taking part in on the BBC. She told me that the Scottish Government would be supporting this and that she would say that SNP MPs would vote for it. No we would not, was my immediate response. There is just no way I could support this legislation. I opposed Labour when they indulged in this anti-civil libertarian nonsense and I will certainly be opposing this Conservative Government as it goes about the same type of business.

Nicola told me that Police Scotland had informed the Government that it needed this legislation to tackle organised crime and fight terrorism. This is a Police Scotland that is led by a former London Met officer who has overseen an organisation that now stops and searches children and routinely arms officers in Highland villages. It would be a huge surprise if they did anything other than want these authoritarian measures. Said to Nicola she cannot count on our support on this and it would be best to give a bland non-answer if it came up. Thankfully it didn't, but waiting for part two of this stand-off between the MP group and our Scottish Government.

Saturday 12 July

T in the Park today and Yes Scotland refused to pay the several thousand of pounds to set up a stall at this Scotland's biggest music festival and gathering of young Scots ahead of the referendum. In what was a total lost opportunity the task of delivering the Yes message was left with the always eager young people in Generation Yes to wander the field with big Yes Saltires. Through huge commitment and perseverance last night they got top Scots band, Biffy Clyro, to take one of these flags onto stage. In a fantastic gesture Yes therefore got on all the coverage and was seen by hundreds of thousands of music fans.

Out and about at the festival today I can see lots of Yes badges and in conversations most of the young, and not so young, people here seem to be Yes supporters. Most Scottish artists are Yes supporters and this is starting to have an impact on their fans. Paolo Nutini and Calvin Harris are performing tonight but we couldn't tempt them to say a few words of encouragement. Having been here before as a musician I know the pressure artists are under from record companies and management to say nothing on political issues. Franz Ferdinand on the other hand had their Yes badges on and went out their way to display their Yes support. That's the way to do it.

Sunday 13 July

It's Sunday that means there must be an opinion poll and indeed there is one from ICM suggesting a 'stalling' or 'flatlining' of support for independence. It shows a 2% fall for support down 36% to 34% from a month ago. While at the same time support for No has gone up 2% to 45%. Twenty-one per cent remain undecided.

When the undecideds are stripped out it leaves a split of Yes 43% and No 57%. Not disastrous by any means but all these polls now suggest that the momentum we were building in the spring has almost certainly stalled and it is quite difficult to determine why. Certainly independence costs, the continued doubts over currency and the threats from business must be having an impact and effect.

There is also something else curious going on and that is the way the canvassing is breaking down with more and more people from working-class communities saying they're voting Yes with bigger difficulties in middle-class areas. In Perthshire we have lots of 'middle-class' voters and they are hard work. We're now at the point of giving up in what is regarded as Tory areas. Also hearing of really good results coming from Glasgow and large towns in West Central Scotland. It certainly feels like the battle lines are reforming in the independence referendum and it looks like the front line will be Labour voters.

Monday 14 July

Called into the weekly SpAd call between the Scottish Government SpAd team and our Westminster staff to discuss the Government's emergency data legislation which will allow for the collection and retention of online data for the UK security services – essentially a precursor to the Tories much-coveted snoopers charter. Chaired by the always affable Geoff Aberdein all key SpAds including Kevin Pringle and Liz Lloyd were on the line. I told them that there is practically no way that the MP group will support this appalling legislation and that it would be pointless trying to get us to change our mind.

There was a half-hearted attempt for us to look at this again with the SpAds concern that we would leave ourselves open to a charge of being soft on crime. There was also Kenny MacAskill's view that we should just support our police efforts almost without question.

Our SpAds are of course Scottish Government staff and they were concerned about the potential embarrassment if we voted against the bill and Kenny's view that we need these powers because the police just happened to tell him that we do. We agreed that I would put forward a recommendation that we would abstain on this legislation to the Westminster group without any real confidence that the group will even touch this compromise with a barge pole. At Westminster I managed to speak to most of the group who were absolutely determined to vote against this bill and saw an abstention as a cop out. Later in the evening I had a conversation with Kenny and communicated this to him where he again tried to get us to change our minds and expressed disappointment with our position. I'm afraid he's just going to have to live with it now!

Tuesday 15 July

At our group meeting we sign up on our approach to today's emergency legislation and we agree that we will oppose. I communicated this to Kevin Pringle who was now resigned to this asking me to say in my speech that we support the principle of the use of personal communication data to help solve crime, which I was happy to comply. In my speech I only get five minutes because of the demand and truncated time we had to deal with this but managed to deliver a rousing though measured contribution to the debate.

After all this build-up and drama practically nobody noticed because today is the start of the biggest Government reshuffle of this Parliament. There are some real shockers, primarily the demotion of Michael Gove, from Education Secretary to Chief Whip and William Hague moving to Leader of the House after announcing he is standing down at the next election.

Meanwhile over in Europe our new best friend Jean-Claude Juncker is letting off a few Euro bombs. Today he has said that there will be no more countries joining the European Union for the next five years. Immediately the Nos are claiming that this would mean we would be out and wouldn't get back in for this five-year period.

Apparently, Juncker had 'slammed the door on Scotland'. Aware that he had inadvertently strayed into the indyref debate a clarifying statement was issued where Juncker stated he was not referring to Scotland. You would have thought that would be the end of it but not a bit of it. So keen are the unionists to have us kicked out of Europe they simply refused to hear and continued to wilfully twist what Juncker said with the usual diet of scare stories and fear and their contention that we would be out.

Wednesday 16 July

Last week we released a Yes video featuring some of our celebrity supporters telling us why they were voting yes. It was a pretty uninspiring piece in which I failed to recognise several of 'our' stars. It also left me wondering what warranted some others' inclusion. Today the Nos launch theirs. Using Queen's 'You're My Best Friend' it was a lot better than ours and much more effective in pulling the heart-strings, the main intention of such pieces. The only thing is, again, I barely recognise many of their 'celebrities' and some that I did recognise were pretty objectionable. There was Ross Kemp, the soap star, who claimed that Glasgow was the most dangerous place on Earth in a piece about gangs only a few years ago. There were the obnoxious style gurus Trinny and Susannah, and for some reason there was the *Blackadder* star Tony Robinson, drawing a turnip in a kilt! With messages of please don't go and undying love declared to us through self-penned billboards it was made for lampoon – and so it very quickly was. The national collective immediately put up a rival Queen song and impromptu video with 'I Want to Break Free' and the boards that these 'stars' were holding were widely rewritten. Great fun.

Walking to college green to do a TV interview I saw that Labour's No bus was parked up outside the House of Lords with loads of Labour MPs queuing to get their photo taken with it. Labour's 'blunder-bus' as I have labelled it is actually quite an effective tool. It has allowed them to have a dynamic centre to their days campaigning and it looks the part. Not sure why it's at Westminster, though, as there are no votes here. Anyway many Labour MPs trying to encourage me to come into their photo. Somehow I don't think that's going to happen.

Thursday 17 July

The First Minister is in Liverpool today on his last speaking engagement in England before the referendum itself. I was wondering why Liverpool until it became apparent later in the day. The former Labour MP for Liverpool Walton, Peter Kilfoyle, a one-time member of Tony Blair's Government, has only come out for Yes. I knew Peter very well when he was an MP and a more principled, decent politician it would be hard to find. He was widely respected by all sides in the Commons and his support is very welcome. In interviews Peter said that independence would benefit the whole of the UK and 'hit out at the "scaremongering" of the No campaign'. He said the Yes campaign was a 'timely reminder' that the English regions have their own issues with an 'overbearing London'.

The FM's main theme in his speech today is about the NHS and how it would not be safe from privatisation if independence is rejected. In a thoughtful and typically Alex way he said that 'Under the Westminster system, cuts to spending in England automatically trigger cuts in Scotland. So if private money replaces public funding in England, our budget will also be slashed, no matter what we want or need.' Adding 'With independence we will have control of both our tax system and budget for public services, so we can protect the NHS and other vital public services from Westminster privatisation.'

Even though it is devolved and under our control with devolution it's been surprising that the NHS has featured so prominently in the indyref with the unionists using it as a symbol of 'British' unity and us now using it about fears for its survival as a public service. Most of our interest in this theme was kick started by a speech from the consultant, Philippa Whitford, whose fantastic speech on the threat to the NHS in the event of a No vote has gone viral with many requests to speak at Yes events. The FM picked this up expertly today and I particularly liked the bit that how an NHS in an independent Scotland could be a positive beacon against continuing privatisation.

Saturday 19 July

We're almost mid-way through the Scottish school summer holiday and you can sense just how quiet it is in the independence debate. After weeks of frenetic full-on campaigning there now seems almost a lull in the activity. Going round the doors there are lots of people away and it also seems that others are taking a break from the debate to enjoy the great weather. We're out in Perth city centre and it's quieter than usual though there are still many people coming to the stall with the most basic of questions or just to be reassured about their Yes vote. Every week now we're cheek by jowl with the No campaign who cower under a Union Jack umbrella and always seem deserted compared to the numbers at our stall. Every town and city centre in Scotland will now have this right up to 18 September and I'm afraid the shoppers will just have to get used to it.

Monday 21 July

The last real day at Westminster before the recess and not sure I will be back here until after the referendum. Westminster returns for the two weeks before the referendum but I, like the rest of my SNP MP colleagues, will be a little bit indisposed. There was all sort of talk that there would be independence themed debates daily on the UK analysis papers but there has been an obvious rethink. I think the UK Government has been wise to dump these plans. Day after day of Westminster Tories giving their own particular tuppence worth on independence could really damage the No case. We are also into the short campaign at that point so that means we would have to get equal time with the broadcasters and how that would be achieved from exclusively unionist Westminster, I don't know. Sure there will be a few independence references during that fortnight but think we'll just let them get on with it.

Tuesday 22 July

Staying in London to finish the filming of my short film on Britishness for Scotland 2014. Quite excited about it and the opportunity to give my opinion on a part of the independence debate that I have made my own. Then it's farewell to all the staff who are now decanting to Scotland. It's now full-on back in Scotland and feel quite excited about getting stuck in round my constituency and really giving it everything. Bye London, love you but hope that our relationship can improve.

Tomorrow is the opening of the Glasgow Commonwealth Games and there has been all sorts of statements and fears about the games being hijacked, by us. Ahead of the Games Glasgow is crammed with senior politicians at a number of events. At a conference of Commonwealth business leaders at the University of Glasgow the First Minister said that he has taken a 'self-denying ordinance not to speak about politics' before adding 'I don't think that, given the vast majority of the 71 countries and territories represented here of course went through the process of becoming independent – just about all of them – think that will be a real worry.' Also there was George Osborne who agreed with the FM that the referendum debate should be kept separate from the Games before saying 'I've set out some of the economic risks that people need to be aware of, but it's very much up to the people of Scotland to make that decision themselves.' We're not even on our 'marks' before the politics is off and running.

Wednesday 23 July

It's the Commonwealth Games opening ceremony but just before the whole thing kicks off Glasgow is being labelled 'Freedom City' by the First Minister, on the back of a prediction that the city will vote Yes. I'm not entirely sure how this fits in with the self-imposed ordinance on speaking about the referendum during the Games and it seems a rather uncharacteristic and curious thing for the FM to say. He of course is criticised for the 'Braveheart' language and how he is 'souring' the Games before they even begin.

David Cameron is also hanging about for the opening ceremony and he also gets stuck in telling us how the Games are 'flying the flag for Britain'. Maybe there should be a gold medal for not bringing up the indyref whilst simultaneously doing everything to ensure you do...

The Games' opening ceremony itself turns out to be a curious in-your-face gallus event that just about gets there. The opening sequence featuring John Barrowman singing about our 'lochs full of monsters' before going through a series of clichés in front of dancing Tunnock's teacakes was just awful. It improved somewhat with performances from Nicola Benedetti and a wonderful version of 'Freedom Come-All-Ye' from a South African opera singer and '500 Miles' from Scottish Ballet. People seemed to enjoy it and if we could just forget about the opening bit it might just have been just about OK. It was not the cultural tour de force of Danny Boyle's Olympic opening but I suppose it could never be on its budget. The designer said it was supposed to be self-deprecating reflecting Glasgow, its humour and its people. It certainly did that.

Thursday 24 July

The big story today is what comes out the back end of a Red Arrow. One of the highlights of the opening ceremony was a flyover by the RAF's Red Arrows who trailed their traditional red, white and blue smoke. During the ceremony I didn't detect any fuss about this but this morning it's hot news. Apparently there was a request for the flight troupe to trail just the blue and white of Scotland as the host country but this was refused. The question that seems to be exciting our friends in the press as to who made the request and who then refused it. The finger of blame, as usual, is being pointed at the First

Minister and the Scottish Government, who today said it was 100% not the case. Pretty unequivocal you would think, particularly when the Games' organisers said it was they who asked for the change to be made.

'But he must have had something to do with it' remains the suspicion from our friends in the press. More interestingly was the response from the new Defence Secretary, Michael Fallon, who seemingly 'reacted with fury' to the request and personally overruled it. This is also disputed with a statement from the Red Arrows backed by the MOD, saying: 'The team represent the UK, we always fly with the red, white and blue'. Cue, all sorts of photos emerging on social media showing the Red Arrows trailing a variety of colours symbolising the events they are appearing at, even one from the opening of the Scottish Parliament where it is, indeed, blue and white. All churlish stuff and a big 'who cares' from the public. But with the Games going on this is what is going to account as a story in the indyref. On the first day of competition sort of wishing it was over already.

Saturday 26 July

With Scotland's Commonwealth success going through the roof we're already detecting a change of mood in the public we're talking to in the indyref campaign. In our usual position in the High Street you could easily detect a new warmth and pride in our nation which is much more open to conversations with us. Where the FM and senior Ministers may have taken a vow of silence we ramp it up in our conversations. So it's a bit 'if we can become such a sporting success we can be huge international success' and 'this is what it's all about Scottish pride and standing up for ourselves'. Goes down well and really hope we get something out of these Games. We need it.

Sunday 27 July

A poll this morning has shown that almost three-quarters of a million Scots would consider leaving the country if there is a Yes vote in September, proclaims the *Sunday Times*. In a Panelbase poll 17%

said they would think about immigrating. The *Times* then did their sums to come up with this incredible figure. Of course there are very few people who believe that will happen but this just helps the whole instability argument in the No camp. In what is not a particularly helpful poll it also finds that 42% said they believe Scotland would be poorer under independence while 34% expected it to be richer. Twenty-eight per cent thought they would be £500 or more a year worse off, while only half of that, at 14%, thought they would be £500 or more better off. In the main question 41% was for Yes with 48% for No vote with 11% undecided. So that's July almost done and we haven't had our breakthrough. If it's going to happen it's going to have to come during the short campaign. We are quickly running out of weeks left and we are not eating into the Nos', as yet, solid lead.

Monday 28 July

A day at the Commonwealth Games as a guest of BP. They invited me along with a few other MPs starting with lunch and ending with an evening of athletics at the refurbished Hampden Park. Glasgow is simply buzzing and I had a good wander round some of the city centre attractions. If we can't build some momentum on the back of this feel-good factor then there is something wrong. The independence referendum has almost vanished and there is practically no politics going on at all. The Scottish people have been glued to their TVs or coming down here to Glasgow which has just recorded one of its busiest weekends ever. In the athletics stadium it is a sea of Saltires and great support for Team Scotland. What is also evident is the support for English athletes even though they were warned that they might get booed. If anything the opposite has happened and it's a great sight to see Scottish fans being so generous with their support. There might be something profoundly interesting emerging here and I think this will be something that will be examined and scrutinised when all this glorious activity comes to an end. It fits in with our new inclusive Scotland narrative that we're building and we must enlist this new feeling.

Tuesday 29 July

My little film for Scotland 2014 on Britishness is on tonight and I am also a guest in the studio to talk about the themes. Got through to Pacific Quay early in the evening to do the last of the voiceovers and see the film for the first time. It looks really good and the interviews I did with Andrew Wilson, Professor James Mitchell and Kate Higgins come across well. Bit anxious about the interview following as I'm sort of on my own with this one as very few other people have tried to take up this theme. I also learn that Scottish Liberal Democrat leader. Willie Rennie, is to be on with me, a heavyweight No figure, obviously deployed to try and close down my argument. The interview in fact goes very well with Willie Rennie having to resort to the traditional negative 'can't do' stuff. Exactly what I wanted out of him. A very good night.

Wednesday 30 July

Taking a total day off today as the whole campaign has almost stopped. Everyone is consumed with the Commonwealth Games and all the independence skirmishes are mostly being ignored. The few indyref stories that are around are connected to the Games with the headlines dominated by things like the woman ejected from the Tollcross International Swimming Centre for waving one of our Yes Saltires. Meanwhile there are Union Jack flags flying anywhere, even though only participating teams' flags should be allowed.

This is apparently OK because we are in the UK and the Union Jack is the UK's flag. There are also double-sided flags being handed out with one side the Saltire and the other the Union Jack, again the suspicion is that they are being handed out by No supporters. I'm really pleased to see that our supporters are not getting unnecessarily wound up by this and going along with it. This is the sort of issue that just bores and frustrates the public and nothing good would come of us making a fuss of it.

Thursday 31 July

Yestival is in Perth tonight. This is a national tour featuring some of the artists involved in the National Collective and they have been on the road for a month from the borders to Shetland and practically everywhere else in between. Perth is the penultimate 'happening' and I'm really pleased to see the Twa Tams full and some local Perthshire artists taking part. Where it's a bit homespun with a slightly eccentric feel to the 'performances' it gets everybody involved and most people seem to have a good time. One thing you could never imagine is the No side doing anything remotely like this. Our young artists have been amongst our most committed supporters and they have enriched the debate and helped shape the Yes movement into a new progressive movement that can only be described as a very positive feature in the new democrat debate.

Just to show that they are making an impact they are constantly being attacked by the press. Today the Spectator blogger and columnist, Alex Massie, has a go at some Scottish writers following the ubiquitous columnist, David Torrance, suggesting that Scottish writers should leave 'politics to the politicians'. On one hand we have practically all of Scotland's young cultural community working flat out to secure our nation's independence and on the other we have all these Tory posh boy, right-wing columnists. Wonder who's going to win that particular popularity contest?

August 2014

Friday 1 August

First thing this morning someone tweeted that the referendum is now next month! If anything was to demonstrate just how imminent it now all was that simple direct tweet summed it up. Just to help us out psephologist supreme, Professor John Curtice, has compiled a 'poll of polls' from the latest six opinion polls, which suggests, perhaps predictably, that the Nos will prevail with 57% would vote No while 43% would vote Yes. According to the good Professor 'Unless Mr Salmond can begin to turn those numbers around, it looks as though Scotland will opt to stay in the Union, albeit perhaps by a margin that some unionists may find rather less than comfortable. The Yes campaign seems to have stalled while still significantly short of its destination.'

Saturday 2 August

It's the Perth Show this weekend and yesterday I got a call from our activists staffing our Yes stall that the UK Government had turned up and had a stall at the show along with the No campaign. I immediately went down to see what was going on, and yes, there they both were, handing out flags and spreading disinformation about the Yes campaign. I concealed my Yes badge and went into speak to one of the UK civil servants who was being paid to put the No case to the show punters. I asked what was the purpose of his presence and didn't they think that one No stall was enough? He gave all this stuff about the UK Government having a position on the referendum and gave me their set of analysis papers, at that point I was revealed as one of these 'nats' and the conversation became a bit more cagey.

The UK civil servants were surprisingly quite verbally aggressive and made no attempt to hide their own particular take on the referendum. Amazing, and just goes to show that the full resource of

Westminster, including their jobbing civil servants are now all fully engaged in fighting the No case. This is certainly going to lead to major problems when we try to put this all together again after 18 September. Got no idea why the pretty insignificant Perth Show warranted the attention of the UK Government but we spent the weekend watching what they were up to and correcting the misinformation they were spreading.

Monday 4 August

Contacted Kevin Pringle about what we're doing to take advantage of the new mood following the Commonwealth Games. The Games has been an overwhelming success and there is real pride in the performance of Scottish athletes. For the past week we have been basking in an unprecedented number of Scottish medals and you can feel that there is a new positive patriotic mood out there just ripe for our taking. We have demonstrated that we can put on a successful huge international event and as a nation we can compete with the best. Surely we should be saying something like we are now winners in Scotland, let's grab the first prize – a country of our own – anything that ties our ambition for our country with the success of our athletes? Surely, we will be saying something like this, and soon? Well no, we wouldn't, certainly not just now, was the reply I got from Kevin. If this was the No side they would be all over this and indeed during the London Olympics we heard nothing else; but such is our reticence to play any sort of patriotic card we will do next to nothing to try and get this to work for us. Everybody thought that the Commonwealth Games may have been one of these fabled game-changers in the indyref debate. Well the way we're playing it we've already dropped the baton.

Tuesday 5 August

For the last few days all indyref debate, discussion and speculation has been about the leaders' debate, which, at last, takes place tonight. This has been set up as some sort of gladiatorial contest and there is a lot at stake and invested in the outcome. This is another of these potential 'game-changers' and everybody has been predicting a 'Salmond win' with the only question being by what sort of margin. Almost sense we were playing down expectations and was actually told off by our SpAd team to ensure that we were not overplaying expectations.

And to the debate and it is an absolute nightmare. You could tell it was going to be bad with the uncharacteristic nervousness of the First Minister and his unusual and disturbing stumbles in his first few contributions. But he'll get better, right? It was also the case that Darling's first few remarks were also not what would be considered cultured and polished. But where Darling settled down into expected assured mediocrity Alex just could not rouse himself. This was bad! Where they got through the first section without any great mishaps or genuine points scored we were all expecting this to be picked up and see the usual First Minister that we all know and love getting stuck in.

Then they got down to the cross-examination where they each got an opportunity to question each other without moderation and suddenly, Darling's making sustained hits with a feeble response from Alex on currency. This was hurting and all Alex could do was to repeat what Darling had said about a currency union from a year ago which just sounded churlish. Surely we would be better prepared on currency than this, and why was Alex not attempting to control the debate?

Then Alex got the chance to question Darling and the first questions were on which side of the road we drive on and some nonsense about alien invasion, what on earth was this? Darling, looking almost relieved at the line of questioning almost exhaled a sigh of relief, with an, is that it? Alex then lost this cross-examination session and therefore the debate. We then went to questions from the audience which is always easiest as you can answer in your own time and always have the last word. This almost felt like a relief after the last hour and a half.

The whole episode had been a disaster and could possibly end any ambition that might still remain of us winning this referendum. There must now be searching questions about who prepared Alex for this and why they decided on such nonsensical flippant questions in the crucial cross-examination session. Still trying to assess what that was all about. In all, Alex just did not look relaxed and just was not himself. Huge opportunity lost, and one that we had to win. It is now going to be hard to come back from this one. The Nos are of course delighted with the performance and an early opinion poll taken after this contest shows that Darling had won. Bad, bad, night from which we may never recover.

I also feature all over social media with my contribution in Scottish Questions when I suggested that Darling vs Salmond would be a 'slaughter worse than the Bannockburn re-enactment'. All the Nos, naysayers and even right-wing columnists taking great delight in reminding me of those now ill-considered remarks. Deserve it I suppose, though in defence it was made before a date was set and we were still in the business of trying to flush Cameron out to debate. Fair play to them, and if it was a 'slaughter' they can probably claim it for themselves.

Wednesday 6 September

All of us in the Yes campaign are wakening up with a massive hangover. Still shell shocked we have probably just lost our last best chance to haul ourselves out of our 5–10 points deficit and at least start to draw equal with the No side. All the headlines are talking about a Darling win this morning and there is a bleak, dark mood round the whole Yes campaign. There are now desperate attempts to try and take comfort from the few crumbs available to us. Desperately, there are press releases from both the SNP and Yes that suggest that the undecideds had come over to our side but it emerges that this is such a small sample size that it is practically pointless, even making us look even more foolish. Looking back at the debate it was clear that Alex just wasn't himself. This is probably down to the pressures of appealing to a variety of audiences. First there were the undecideds, then there are women voters who we are told don't like what is described as his 'smug' demeanour, then there would be advice about speaking direct to a television audience. He should of course just have been himself. There's no doubt all the competing tensions about how he should come across affected his performance. Let Alex be Alex, for goodness sake. Then there is the currency. How we weren't properly prepared for this I don't know. We must have known that their case would be practically all about this but yet we were buffeted and blown all over the place. Today there is a clamour that we now reveal our Plan B for currency all over again and this has extended beyond the usual commentators and No supporters. We have put ourselves in a very bad place on currency and it is now too late to address the fundamental and critical flaws in our approach. We need a better answer than last night, and we need it fast.

The first of my 'Yes in the Square' today where I am taking a soapbox and a host of musicians to the village and town squares of Perthshire plus a huge double-decker bus adorned in Yes regalia. We're starting in Blairgowrie and it's all a bit of a wing and a prayer and a great deal of hope. Typically it starts late and verging on shambolic but we turned it around. I had Alan (Citizen) Smart with his referendum songs and I gave this passionate case for the union out of the very loud PA system. It actually worked and it went down well in both Coupar Angus and Alyth where we headed off to next.

Thursday 7 August

No sign of the debate fallout disappearing today if anything the headlines are even worse. There is talk of Alex's authority in the SNP and there was a group meeting in the Scottish Parliament amongst the SNP MSPs where it is said that Alex gave a passionate contribution with many wondering why he didn't do it the other night? Today is also the first First Minister's Questions of a Scottish Parliament returned early to fit in a break for the referendum campaign. All three leaders predictably went on the pound and in response Alex was a bit more secure and started to bring in the issue of debt saying again that if we don't get the assets we don't have any responsibilities for the liabilities. He also questioned whether it would be wise to question 'the sovereign will' of the Scottish people which is a new one. Finally the pound was as much ours as it was anybody else's on these isles and we will not be denied its use. This is a bit more like it but it is not enough to cover up our deep difficulties on the currency issue.

I suppose we only have ourselves to blame. On currency they control the debate. They can simply say they will not allow a currency union and continue to ask what is our plan B in the face of their refusal. Our inability to give one makes our case look weak and that we have something to hide. We can do nothing now but tough it out even with Jim Sillars saying that 'for the life of me' he can't understand why we can't just propose our own currency. There's a lot of people in Yes now wondering why we didn't go with that one. Particularly as it would mean that we would not be beholden to them for agreement and arrangement.

The love bombing has started. A letter has appeared this morning signed by 200 various UK celebrities described as a 'love letter to Scotland'. In it they say 'Let's stay together… what unites us is greater than what divides us'.

It is the usual and predictable sort of 'stick together' message but it is effective because it remains just that without going into sermonising or being patronising. There are some very impressive and respected names on the list, people like Stephen Hawking and David Attenborough. Huge stars like Mick Jagger and Sting and popular ever-presents like Bruce Forsyth and Cilla Black. There are also a lot of names that no-one will have heard of and some who curiously have form in disparaging and insulting Scotland in the past.

Arranged by Dan Snow and Tom Holland it is a pretty well organised and affectionate initiative which is well presented by Dan Snow in the interviews I saw him conduct. It won't make much difference as no-one in Scotland is paying attention to this type of stunt anymore and there is a general sense that this is now Scotland's decision and we just want to be left to get on with it. This could have been huge if it was deployed a bit earlier and at a less congested time in the debate. The Nos have made a real mess of their 'love bombing' campaign and they certainly are not going to secure anything like the impact seen in Quebec where the equivalent No campaign deployed this so effectively.

Friday 8 August

With the gaping wound on our currency stand the unionists are going in for the kill. Today Ed Miliband is in Scotland and on morning radio I hear him say that he will even include a commitment to rule out a currency union in the next Labour manifesto. All day it is about a 'plan B' and even in our canvassing last night we were finding that our undecided voters were looking a bit more shaky over our less than convincing arguments about currency. Meanwhile we are sticking to our argument that the UK will simply change its mind after a Yes vote and wouldn't bring such economic havoc on itself by refusing a currency union. The ferocity of the hardline adopted by the UK parties is growing in intensity with Miliband even saying that he knows ruling out a currency union would hurt the disadvantaged in Scotland but he would rule it out anyway. This is now beginning to look like the economic bullying that accompanied George Osborne's initial statement on currency. The only hope we've got is that the indignation that accompanied the Chancellor's first forays into sharing the pound will reappear. Got the feeling that this time we are all indignant-ed out.

Saturday 9 August

First opinion poll since the debate and predictably it's bad. Where all of us must have anticipated that the first opinion poll after the Commonwealth Games and leaders' debate would have given us some comfort it is instead giving us even more cause for concern. It is in the *Mail* and it has the almost joyous headline that the No campaign has 'more than doubled its lead' compared to the last

Survation poll it commissioned. It places No on 50%, Yes on 37% with the undecideds 13%. It found 'viewers overwhelmingly believed that Better Together leader Mr Darling crushed his opponent' in the TV debate with a quarter of those who watched now 'more likely' to vote against independence. The only shred of comfort is that it shows that undecideds are at 33% which we are desperately translating that it is 'all to play for'. This of course is no surprise can only be described as being one of the worst weeks we have experienced in the campaign. And what a time to do it – six weeks out of the referendum itself.

Sunday 10 August

Still no respite from our currency woes. All the papers keen to keep this going and it continues to dominate everything in the indyref campaign. The *Sunday Herald* features a particularly passionate response from the First Minister where he attacks the No campaign for its 'obsession' with a Plan B saying 'Implicit in that formulation is settling for what is second-best, and in this case what would be second-best for Scotland.' He repeats the view that 'it's our pound and we are keeping it'. Meanwhile a Survation poll has a four-point increase in the No vote since the television debate. The poll places No on 50%, Yes on 37% and undecided on 13%. Stripping out the 'don't knows' No has 57% of the vote, Yes has 43%. It also (helpfully) has a breakdown of the adjectives most associated with Salmond and Darling during the debate. Salmond's are 'weak' (18%), 'uninformed' (13%), while Darling had 'knowledgeable' (21%) and 'strong' (16%). Who would ever have thought that type of outcome even remotely possible?

The referendum was always probably going to be lost but last week was when we could more or less concede that is all but confirmed. We are probably playing for the best possible defeat now. Getting over 45% will now be a very good result which will allow us to keep the concept of independence in play and keep the party in reasonably good health. Forty to 45% would now seem like a reasonable day at the office where we could claim a creditable performance and just get on with making the most of the post-referendum world. If, however, it is below 40% we could be in for a bit of trouble. This would be seen as a decisive defeat that could lead to internal difficulties in the party and a mass depression amongst all those who have given everything in the campaign. I know colleagues must now be looking at these scenarios and many of us (after this long campaign) are beginning to look beyond the referendum and not many of us are starting that task based on a decisive Yes vote and a move towards independence. Hopefully we can still get into the 40s. That's seems like what we are playing for now.

Monday 11 August

Another opinion poll out this morning in *The Sun* and I knew it was going to be bad when the over-enthusiastic No-supporting political editor, Kevin Schofield, seemed to be very much looking forward to publishing it. Today we find that No is on 55%, Yes on 35% with the undecided on 11%. Once the 'Don't Knows' are excluded, No has 61% with Yes on 39%, a lead of 22 points. Right now it seems to be getting worse and worse but even with all this it seems we are almost blotting it all out and questioning the poll. Sort of going where madness leads to just now.

Remarks made yesterday by Boris Johnson seem to be picking up this morning when he said that there is 'No need to give Scots more powers' – stating that the comments 'undermine the consensus' at Westminster for giving Holyrood extra powers following a 'No' vote in September. Boris is everybody's favourite to lead the Tories after Cameron and there is even polling to show that the Conservatives would be comfortably in the lead if Boris was in charge. Not sure his popularity writ extends to Scotland and he is one of the few leading No figures who constantly suggests constraining our powers and looking at our spending arrangements. His intervention could be useful.

Tuesday 12 August

All about women today or at least our difficulties in convincing them of a Yes vote. Apparently, women are less likely to support independence because they are more uncertain about the future, according to a new analysis out today. This is the report by ScotGen, a social research institute who in a paper, titled 'Mind the Gap', shows that whilst 43% of men intend to vote Yes, only 31% of women intend to vote for independence. It also found that the biggest gender difference was in the 'don't know' category – 19% of women surveyed said they were unsure, whilst 10% of men had not made their minds up.

This is something we are finding in our canvassing. On the doorstep we can find the male partner a convinced Yesser while his partner is full of doubts. There are issues about Alex, the fact that many women don't like him, and there are also issues about what is seen to be a historically masculine campaign based on old and redundant, images of Scottish patriotism and Braveheart-ism, or even support for the national football side. We are therefore caught in a curious tension of trying to soften the image to attract women while compromising a more passionate resonance to garner 'soft patriots' to Yes. It looks like we might have got this wrong by half-heartedly chasing both at the same time while blunting the message to each.

Another feature of this study found that the Scottish people are now feeling more British since the referendum campaign started. Asked to rank their Scottishness against their Britishness, only 26% said they were 'more Scottish than British', the lowest figure since the survey began in 1992. I would like to think this is down to my work in trying to secure a British vote for Yes but suspect that those who have hardened up as No supporters are less reticent and shy in describing themselves as British.

Thursday 14 August

We've tried to get the Scottish people to look at the threat to our NHS with a No vote and it looks like it is at last having some effect. We get the sense it is working because of the howls of protests from Unionist politicians who are pretty indignant about this claiming that the NHS is fully devolved. Where the Nos are right that it is indeed under the Scottish Parliament's operational control we have raised the funding of the NHS and the threat to our service with the privatisation agenda being pursued south of the border. Our case has been that for every £100 lost in public spending in health care to private funding south of the border £10 is lost in Scotland in Barnett consequential spending. They do not like this at all and have been howling 'scaremongering' at us. Fantastic, they now know how it feels!

Where it is not the most convincing of cases (spending on health has actually increased in England) we have made the threat of planned privatisation almost stick. Maybe if we had been a bit more 'negative' with some of these issues we could have had a bit more resonance with a public always concerned about the future of the NHS. But such is our commitment to fight a wholly positive campaign we wouldn't countenance a more negative approach.

At the Edinburgh Festival today taking in a few shows. I used to be a regular attender and lapped the whole event up, nowadays my visits are more of the fleeting variety. Where the International Festival was keen not to have the event dominated by the indyref the Fringe is full of it and there are any number of shows on exploring the referendum, almost overwhelmingly from a Yes perspective. In total contradiction to the fears that comedians were reticent about involving themselves with the indyref there are plays from Alan Bissett, David Hayman and David Greig's *All Back to Bowie's*, a great title following the invitation from the great man for Scotland to 'stay with us' at the BRITS. Throughout the day I bump into Hardeep Singh Kolhi who has an indy show on, as well as Perth comic Bruce Fummey. Great day and only wish I could get down more.

Sunday 17 August

What is it with the indyref? Just when you think it is all done and dusted something comes along that makes you question your judgement and certainty. Today, two opinion polls have arrived which show an increase for Yes and there is a few of us thinking – where on earth did this come from?

The polls are in both the *Sunday Herald* and *Scotland on Sunday*. *The Herald*'s is a Panelbase poll commissioned by us that has Yes on 48% and No on 52% when the don't knows are excluded. In *Scotland on Sunday* it is an ICM poll putting Yes on 45% and No on 55%, the highest we have ever been with that polling organisation. Absolutely incredible after the week we have had and the polls have hardly been tighter. Trying to figure out what is going on in the indyref is now becoming nothing other than untested speculation and the twists and turns like an out-of-control electoral roller coaster.

The resilience of the Yes campaign is quite extraordinary. The way we have withstood setbacks but still remain there or thereabouts, remarkable. It should be all but over but we're still snapping at their heels. Even in the face of adversity there remains a cast iron certainty in the Yes camp and the discipline has been like something out of the SAS. More and more people are out campaigning, more conversations are being had and more information and literature is being distributed. Is the grassroots campaign having a bigger impact than we thought possible? Are we circumnavigating the press and the mainstream debate and securing an audience uninterested in the big campaign themes such as currency?

The Nos have certainly talked of nothing other than currency for the past week, as they would, but it is getting close to the lecturing and hectoring tone of George Osborne's early intervention – is this having a negative impact for the Nos? Nothing seems clear this morning though the polls have been met with a sense of relief and almost euphoria within the Yes campaign. Does this mean we might now win? Well, let's take it easy... It doesn't, and we have still never been ahead in any poll, and we needed to see one credible poll showing us ahead before the schools go back. It does mean that it will go right down to the wire and the Nos will now be unsure about their expected decisive victory. It is also enough for us to believe that we don't need to change strategy and will probably do nothing to recalibrate our campaign and just chip away with the usual themes and the core message of logical and safe unemotional independence. This will panic the Nos, though, and we can expect them to up their campaign this week determined to try and knock us back down again. But sitting here this morning it is difficult to know where they can actually take their campaign now.

Scotland's top historian, Tom Devine, has come out in support of independence. This is important as Devine is universally respected and his position as our top historian almost undisputed. He is also a thoroughly nice man who has been engaged in Scotland's civic debate for decades throughout his illustrious career. There may be endorsements from all sorts of celebrities but this is a weighty intervention. He has said he has recently switched from the 'No' camp to the 'Yes' camp because he has realised the Union has run its course. He commented that the union was a 'marriage of convenience' not love and that Scots are 'wedded to a social democratic agenda' while the English have 'embarked on a separate journey'. It actually feels good to be on the same side as people such as Tom Devine.

Monday 18 August

It's exactly one calendar month till the indyref and yet another milestone to be marked as the decisive day comes ever closer. The Scottish cabinet are meeting in Arbroath to make their clumsily titled 'declaration of opportunity'. I've got no idea who comes up with such awful slogans but it doesn't seem they've been up all night thinking of this one!

Absolutely reeking of symbolism I hear the First Minister all too obviously attempt to link this to the original Declaration of Arbroath. With the success of last week's campaign on the NHS the 'declaration' will include that a Scottish NHS remains in public hands as well as similarly meaningless commitments. The issue of currency is still not going away and Alex is still not sounding all that certain on this yet. Today he said something curious about trade unionists not saying what they would settle for in negotiations with management. Yesterday on a radio phone he also came as close as he could to admitting he wasn't up to par at last week's debate saying he wishes he had explained his position on currency a bit more clearly. I've known Alex for the best part of 20 years and I have never known him so uncertain and unsure as he is sounding just now. Maybe the constant personalising of the campaign round him and the demonising he has had to endure by the Nos and the press is having an impact. We need him at his very best just now but he just sounds tired. Maybe just take a couple of days off and be fighting fit for the last few weeks.

There's also another opinion poll out this morning from our favourite pollster, YouGov, and again even with them we are up, in fact it shows that our support has risen four points in a week. Even with this increase, YouGov (being the worst pollster for a Yes vote) still only find us at 43% with the Nos at 57% but believe it or not this is the highest the Yes vote has polled in a YouGov survey since the beginning of the referendum campaign. Almost as helpfully, and perhaps something that helps explain the resilience of the Yes support, it found that 44% thought that Westminster politicians were bluffing over claims there would be no currency union, while 40% believed them. Forty-five per cent of those polled supported a currency union with the rest of the UK.

Tuesday 19 August

It's approaching something akin to trench warfare just now in the indyref with both sides hunkered down in their respective trenches. The Nos continue to pummel our lines with the currency howitzers whilst we throw the grenades marked 'NHS privatisation'.

Today on currency, the debate is joined by two former Chief Executives of Scottish Enterprise, Jack Perry and Crawford Beveridge, the former being on the No side and the latter the former chair of the FM's Fiscal Commission. The First Minister is giving further hints about 'sterlingisation' even saying it might be a transitional arrangement delighting the Nos who are asking, transitioning to what? Meanwhile Crawford Beveridge said: 'We remain firmly of the view that a well-designed monetary union is the best option for both Scotland and the UK post-independence.' While Jack Perry, said: 'If [the plan] is just to use the pound anyway without a currency union, as they hint at, there would be serious consequences for Scotland's public services. Scotland would have to run a fiscal surplus – cutting spending and increasing taxes – to have the cash to make that plan work.'

These shells may keep pouring down but we're increasingly well dug in now. Meanwhile in the Scottish Parliament, in a bad-tempered debate, the NHS is discussed. The Nos are totally overreacting to this demonstrating that this is gaining traction out there. Surprised at how easily wound up by this the Nos have become we will now dig away at this for the next few weeks. We might not have the armoury of the Nos but our little arsenal is having an effect.

Wednesday 20 August

The BBC has made a curious reappearance today with all sort of No claims about popular programmes not being available if we dare to vote Yes. This was all kicked off by the former BBC Director General who has warned that the national broadcaster may lose up to a quarter of its funding if Scotland votes for independence and that our plans to work with the BBC is 'make believe'. Boldy asserting that 'One way or another, after independence, Scottish viewers would have to pay to receive BBC services.' Today this theme is picked up by Labour's Shadow Scottish Secretary, Margaret Curran who reinforces that we would miss out on important programmes. Where there are issues with our broadcasting plans international experience shows that we can simply buy the BBC programmes we want with the excess in our own licence fee, a cursory look at the arrangements in Ireland clearly show that. We also want to work in partnership with the BBC and would see this as a sensible way forward. This doesn't matter though as it is a cute scary comeback after our NHS hits. The thing is that the Scottish people have been closely watching the BBC throughout this referendum and have seen many of its shortcomings. Maybe a threat to the BBC doesn't seem as existential as it once was.

Friday 22 August

One of the 'bravest' things we did in the early days of the referendum campaign was to say we would secure a million signatures for our independence pledge. Alex Salmond even went as far to say that if a million signatures were reached we would win our independence. The unionists, of course, said that it couldn't be done and they scoffed and dismissed the whole exercise. Well today it has been achieved. I have to admit that I was quite sceptical of the exercise and thought it was a hostage to fortune and had more or less forgotten all about 'the pledge'. But fair play this looks rather good and encouraging. Yes Scotland even has the Proclaimers there with Yes campaigners and all round everyone is looking pleased with themselves. Will it change anything? Well probably not, but it shows that even the 'slow burners' in this campaign can still bear fruit.

Sunday 24 August

For a Sunday it's all about tomorrow with the build-up to the last of the televised referendum debates. The second and last TV debate between Alistair Darling and Alex Salmond, will be tomorrow at Glasgow's Kelvingrove Museum and broadcast live throughout the UK. After the last debate Alex is actually considered the underdog and most commentators are saying that Alex needs a 'knock-out blow' if he is to rescue the Yes campaign. Most of the Nos are trying to play down expectations about Alistair Darling suggesting that Alex will come out stronger this time. Darling's unexpected victory stunned all of us in the Yes camp and it took a lot of energy out of the Yes campaign. The build-up to this debate is therefore a bit unnerving for us who are more than aware what is resting on this. Everybody I spoke to out canvassing today intends to watch the debate and this is taking on gladiatorial proportions. There are many remarkable things about this referendum campaign and the spectator sport of a political debate is just another one of them.

Monday 25 August

It's all about the second debate today and everybody is speculating on who will win and what will be raised. Everybody expecting Darling to go on the economy and sterling with the FM advised to 'go negative to save his dream of independence'. In the papers it's all a 'last opportunity' for Salmond with the 'Yes camp still trailing'. A source close to the First Minister predicts the debate will not be a 'slugging match'. We're told that the First Minister will concentrate on a conversational approach and address the electorate, rather than be confrontational with Darling.

After tonight there is nothing else, there are no set-piece debates, no major announcements, just campaigning. If Alex loses it is game over, a narrow win makes no difference, only something approaching a knock-out blow can make any difference to our current perilous condition. Rushing back from the now nightly canvass session it was almost akin to watching from behind the sofa stuff.

But this is good. Immediately you can see from Alex's demeanour he's up for this. His opening statement hits all the right buttons and he's confident and assertive. Darling fumbles, blinks furiously and looks nervous and hesitant. This is better. Alex dominating the debate and coming out from the lectern to address the audience directly. Alex also decides to raise the issue of currency himself and it's all about the themes he tested last week – if we vote Yes it will be the 'sovereign will' of the Scottish people, talks of the debt as part of the settlement. He challenges Darling to say what would be the best currency option for an independent Scotland, under pressure Darling even says that Scotland could use the pound, to shrieks of derision.

The cross-examination is the usual rammy but this time Alex takes no hostages and asks Darling to list three job-creating powers Scotland would get if we voted No, which he can't. Darling is at his most vulnerable in having to defend an unelected Tory Government, claiming he is a 'Labour politician'. Towards the end Darling just wilted, wishing it was over. It was a slaughter worse than the Bannockburn re-enactment, as I so inelegantly put it a few weeks ago.

The immediate, and now obligatory, debate exit poll shows the scale of the victory. Seventy-one per cent says Salmond won the debate, 29% Darling. This is fantastic and could be significant. All the commentators are also giving it to Alex and he was very good tonight. He did this because he came out as himself and was unafraid to turn negative and persistent when required. Everybody in Yes will be happy with tonight's performance and we will see how this now plays out on the doorsteps.

Tuesday 26 August

Papers full of the referendum debate and it is all good for the Yes campaign. All the papers agree that Alex clearly bettered Darling and even the Better Together campaign found very few if any positives from it. It was either 'a combative cross-examination of Darling' in which he asked, 'Why are you standing here defending Conservative policies on a joint platform with the Conservatives?' Many papers concluded that 'It was his chance to make the case his independence dream directly to hundreds of thousands of voters in their living rooms – and he seized it with both hands.'

Perhaps predictably the *Daily Mail* said 'An arrogant and unstatesmanlike First Minister bullied his way through the most important 90 minutes of his political career.' We are all feeling buoyed by the debate and the mood from a few weeks ago could not be more different. It's strange how much an impact these debates have on the perception on the campaign and today Alex was once again challenging Cameron to debate. On the doorstep the conversations were full of it. Many didn't like the combative nature of the exchange but those who did make a judgement concluded that they agreed with the First Minister on most of the issues.

A quite extraordinary referendum broadcast from the Nos hit the screen tonight that literally had our jaws hitting the floor. It was a mother and housewife dizzily talking directly to camera listing all the reasons why she hadn't had the time to make up her mind about the referendum before, of course, making up her mind to vote No. There were references to preparing the children's breakfast with an 'eat your cereal' refrain whilst expressing a boredom with the whole debate. This was someone so disconnected from the debate that she didn't even know who the First Minister was! An incredible broadcast that seemed to come straight out of the 1950s when politics was left to men and women didn't have the time to worry about that sort of stuff.

The response from social media was immediate and damning. The woman was branded the 'patronisingBTlady' and Twitter was soon awash with spoof videos. I have absolutely no idea why the Nos chose this particular approach with practically every opinion poll showing they have a commanding lead in the crucial women's vote. This patronising twaddle could only lose them support amongst women and this broadcast has been an uncharacteristic mistake from a campaign that has barely put a foot wrong in recent weeks. It will also create massive problems from amongst the many female politicians in the Labour Party who have made equality issues their life work and will be watching this with something approaching horror. Now, go eat your cereal...

Wednesday 27 August

We're all trying to suppress our guffaws as Gordon Brown at last shares a stage with Alistair Darling tonight. Apparently they're putting aside their famous differences for their beloved union. Their uncomfortable reunion is overshadowed though in the shape of Archie Macpherson. The 79-year-old legendary sports commentator has had enough and he declares he 'couldn't stand it any longer' and felt compelled to speak out against 'the obfuscation and evasion streaming out of the independence campaign'. In what must rank as one of the best No speeches of the campaign he puts to shame the professional politicians with real passion to rapturous applause from the mobbed Dundee Caird Hall. This is what the Nos have needed all along. People who actually care about their union giving it how they feel unfettered by political concerns. I certainly hope the Nos don't find any more Archies...

Last word about the debate today with a number of unionists crying foul and even Better Together lodging complaints with the BBC. Their claim is that all the questions seemed to favour the First Minister with even the suggestion that BBC audience favoured Yes. All barking stuff and the irony meter going off scale after the soft ride the unionists have had from the BBC. Maybe we'll see them protesting outside Pacific Quay soon.

Thursday 28 August

The Prime Minister is back in Scotland with a speech to the CBI. This has proved to be more noteworthy than usual because the CBI is, of course, no longer a registered organisation and has to be careful on how much it can now spend. They were expected to have splashed out on a lavish doo but have been warned by the Electoral Commission. Cue all sort of gags about the prawn cocktail and arctic roll menu awaiting Dave. His appearance turns out to be a PR disaster when his speech is overshadowed by embarrassing criticism from Sir Michael Rake, the leader of the CBI. Before Cameron's speech Sir Michael said that the uncertainty surrounding the status of an EU referendum and a possible withdrawal from the EU by the UK was damaging business. Totally humiliating for Cameron whose central message was about how the UK would offer 'certainty, stability and predictability'. This of course just reminds the Scottish people that our real EU difficulties come from remaining in the UK, the last thing Cameron wanted on this trip. Pretty sure that the menu didn't get any sweeter following that blunder.

As if things couldn't get any worse for Dave as one of his MPs has just defected to UKIP announcing a by-election. The rather odd and eccentric, Douglas Carswell, has finally accepted the Farage shilling and has caused a political storm. Cameron's CBI disaster has only gone and been overshadowed by something much worse.

Friday 29 August

My 'good friend' Jim Murphy has been touring the streets of Scotland with a soap box and a microphone in what he grandly called his 100 streets in 100 weeks tour. When he started it was just one angry man shouting at the few souls who bothered to turn up for his rants, usually bemused Yes voters. But with increasing publicity Yes campaigners have been turning up in greater numbers just for a bit of sport. Today he was hit with an egg and it is all over the papers and media. Watching the scene on TV it was more Keystone Cops than Gunfight at the OK Corral.

On the mean streets of downtown Kirkcaldy, after deftly dodging a number of eggs heading in his direction, his 'assailant' took no more chances and with a second carton of eggs proceeded to throw an egg at point-blank range breaking all over Murphy's white shirt.

The Nos typically, and with some real justification, at last, went to town. At a hastily arranged press call Murphy revealed, 'We've been in contact with the Police to discuss safety because Yes Scotland have organised mobs to turn up at these meetings, and tried to silence people'. After months of telling us about the nastiness and intimidation of Yes supporters they now had real evidence of the scale of the problem in the shape of an egg. Why on earth we couldn't just stay well away and let him get on with his inconsequential rant, I don't know, but the Nos have finally been able to get their proof of the aggression and intimidation at the heart of the Yes campaign.

In Perth I was on an unusual and even heartwarming panel when the Perth-based homeless charity CATH organised a hustings for Perth's homeless community and those attending other voluntary agencies assisting people with homelessness, mental health and substance abuse.

We've been hearing a lot about how those amongst our most vulnerable and marginal in Scotland want to participate in the referendum and there have been all sorts of stories about queues at electoral registration offices in advance of next week's cut off. That's why for this hustings I asked someone from the electoral registration office in Perth to come along and advise anyone who still wishes to vote next month how they could still get on the register.

Incredibly the place is packed to the gunnels with a real interest in the debate and fantastic questions and participation. The indyref has gripped every sector of our community and when I asked how many intended to vote practically every hand went up. This audience were overwhelmingly if not exclusively for Yes (it would be pretty hard for people at the most marginal in our society to support a status quo) and it would be nigh impossible to imagine this interest or participation in a standard political contest. People now increasingly believe that our independence could transform our society completely and those who have dismissed previous contests as a – 'you're all the same' – see a real opportunity with independence. Just hope we can live up to that expectation if we are indeed successful.

First opinion poll since the debate and it is very good. Coming from the *Daily Mail* the accompanying headline is 'Union on a Knife Edge' and this is apparently because a Survation poll has No at 53% and Yes on 42%. There is no doubt that there is a new mood emerging following the debate and the Yes side is feeling more energised and there is a new confidence out there. Canvassing has been quite remarkable and we are now revisiting undecideds and finding them now coming over to us. If timing is everything then this is a very good time to get some momentum building. This is only one opinion though and we will have to wait and see the polls due over the weekend

Saturday 30 August

Out at our stall on Perth High Street today and the atmosphere is electric. We actually run out of badges and posters and there is a constant procession of people asking questions. We really are on the home straight of the campaign and everybody is wanting to have discussions and conversations about independence and what it could mean. People are totally engaged and I have never seen excitement in politics like this before. As a practising politician this is just something remarkable and it feels like another country.

Go up to the Birnam Highland Games in the afternoon and we have a stall on the way in and it is similarly going like a fair. Lots of international visitors stopping for a chat and to find out a little more about the campaign. Inside, people are asking me for badges and Yes wristbands and the conversations never stop. There are people I have known for years who have previously expressed a No opinion who are now fervent Yes voters. There's something almost in the air just now and if we could only bottle it.

Jim Murphy has now postponed his tour citing 'security' issues. He claims he is seeking police advice. This just keeps the story running and keeps attention on all the supposed hostility and negativity in the Yes campaign. Objective achieved by Jim.

Sunday 31 August

For all the things that are going on just now it is surprisingly a relatively quiet Sunday. Looks like the biggest story is Paul McCartney supporting the Nos, but it looks like even Macca can't save the Nos' disastrous handling of their 'love bombing' campaign. The way that the Scots people have not been seduced by the approaches of these UK celebrities will be one of the biggest stories of the indyref.

Meanwhile we continue to attract all sorts of Scottish artists and musicians to the cause. This morning I saw a YouTube video of Del Amitri's, Justin Currie, filling out his postal vote. Justin has been one of the most anti-Yes musicians of my generation of musicians but in this video he hits out at the scare campaign of the Nos before putting his cross next to Yes. This will have more impact than any English-based celeb and there is even an annoyance factor creeping in about being told what to do from our friends south of the border.

September 2014

Monday 1 September

We can now talk about 'this month's' referendum. It is now September 2014 and this will go down as one of the most important months in Scottish political history. The energy is building and the excitement is almost tangible. The only thing trying to dampen it down is the return to one of the favourite themes of the Nos, all the 'intimidation' and 'bullying'. Today they're raising concerns about the security arrangements around polling day. Apparently there are claims that Police Scotland are considering stationing more police at polling stations, in order to safeguard against 'high tensions and flashpoints' associated with the predicted high turnout.

This is all in response to the almost blanket coverage of Jim Murphy's soap box postponement which he predictably restarted today in another blaze of publicity. Alex, particularly good in an interview comparing Murphy to 'a religious zealot on a soap box'. He suggested that voters stay away from Murphy's pro-Union campaign speeches, saying: 'If Mr Murphy comes bawling and shouting on a street corner near you any time soon keep doing your shopping, keep doing what you were doing. He's just like the guy with "The End is Nigh" round his neck; he'll go away soon.'

I'm chairing a Question and Answer session with Alex in Perth tonight. We got word on Friday that Alex wanted to start his Q and A tour round Scotland in Perth and we were of course delighted to oblige. Given the short notice we weren't sure if we'd get a crowd but there were actually queues to get in with people rammed into the Salutation Hotel with standing room only.

Alex was on top form and the place was captivated. It also took him about an hour to get away with everybody wanting autographs and 'selfies'. His team told me exactly the same thing happened in

Dundee this afternoon when he addressed a joint meeting of Dundee and Dundee United fans. This is real rock star treatment and Alex does this so well. Where it's true that Alex divides opinion people want to see him and hear from him. A fantastic night and it has certainly helped motivate our support in Perth.

Tuesday 2 September

At last night's meeting Alex gave me word of a fantastic opinion poll from YouGov that would appear this morning and fantastic it is. Basically, our worst pollster, YouGov, has the gap between Yes and No vote down to six points, 53–47. The same poll last month had this gap at 14 points. This morning it is absolute bedlam and a real sense of crisis in the response from the Nos. All the press are saying things like 'A close finish looks likely, and a Yes victory is now a real possibility' and 'If No finally wins the day, it now looks less likely that it will win by a big enough margin to deliver a knock-out blow to supporters of independence.' I head down to London for my cover duties at Westminster and the place in a strange mood. Tory MPs come up to me and ask is it true – 'might we lose'? I confirm gravely (for them) that is now a real possibility. Westminster just does not know how to respond. It has lost its swagger. No-one will be 'bayoneting the wounded' anymore. Westminster doesn't know whether to despair, hit out, bribe, bully, or just stay right out of it.

What is happening with the Nos publicity? Last week there was that awful 'patronising lady' broadcast and today they have released a poster campaign which boldly says that 'We love our kids. We're saying No Thanks'. The inverse inference therefore must be – if you don't love your kids you vote Yes. Almost outrageous in its audacity it is already getting pelters. Nicola got it on the money when she said 'The No campaign has learned absolutely nothing from their disastrous TV broadcast last week – not content with patronising women, they're now patronising all of Scotland's voters and their families. We all love Scotland and we all love our families.' Where you always have to take a bit of a risk with the publicity the Nos almost seem to have gone out of their way to antagonise. Saatchi's are notionally in charge of the No publicity contract and I'm presuming that a few harsh words are being shared.

Thursday 4 September

Ed Miliband is back in town and we are invited to believe that Scotland doesn't need to worry about the union because he's set to become Prime Minister! Describing the Conservatives as 'defecting, divided and downhearted' he makes the bold claim 'the Tories are on their way out'. Ed was done a favour in one of the now almost nightly debates when Scottish Conservative leader, Ruth Davidson, in an almost desperate piece of reassurance, said that a Conservative Government was 'unlikely'.

The thing is on the doorstep practically no-one believes that there is even the remote possibility of a Prime Minister Miliband, and former Labour voters almost laugh when you suggest it. Labour hope to win the general election with some 35% of the UK vote but the problem for them, is even if they do, they will have to govern with almost 50% of the electorate opting for either the Tories or UKIP. Labour know that there are issues for them up here. Increasing number of Labour voters are now moving to Yes and there is an almost unbridgeable gap being built up between the Labour leadership and its now former voters. There is no doubt as a party Labour are being hurt by their association with the Tories in Better Together and their credibility amongst their core voters stretched to almost breaking point.

Friday 5 September

A bad, bad day today, which is all my own fault. All week we have been trying to sense how many MPs will be about for a vote on a Private Members' Bill which partly deals with some issues around the bedroom tax. Private Members' Bills usually don't illicit much attention or excitement but Andrew George's Affordable Homes Bill has attracted quite a bit of mail in my inbox. Where Andrew's Bill exempts some vulnerable groups it does not abolish the bedroom tax and like all bills opposed by the Government it is doomed to be lost in committee. What it does do is propose exceptions to particular groups, things we are already doing in Scotland, with the mitigation measures introduced by the Scottish Government.

In the run up to the referendum all of my colleagues want to be up in Scotland campaigning and we all have commitments in our constituencies. We therefore decide that Eilidh Whiteford and Mike Weir will stay down and cover and Mike would make a speech. I would also be on stand-by if required to come down to vote. Mike would phone me first thing in the morning if it looks like it's going to a close vote or if it is particularly busy.

Disastrous planning! First thing in the morning we learn that it is teeming and even Alistair Darling and Gordon Brown are there. I'm immediately out the door and enlist Stewart Hosie who I meet at the airport. This was all going to be extremely tight. At the airport we discover there is a slight delay on our flight but still manageable for an anticipated 2.30pm vote. Then I get a call to say that a 'closure' motion was to be introduced early meaning we had no chance of getting there in time. Stewart and I decide to return home.

I watch the vote on TV and my heart sinks when I see practically all the Scottish Labour MPs there. Checking with the staff they identify all 41 Scottish Labour MPs present and correct. Is there a chance they might not notice our absence? No, not a chance whatsoever, and my Twitter feed is soon choked with No supporters berating me for not showing up. My phone is red hot with journalists demanding to know why I wasn't there and my honesty was even being questioned when I said I tried to make it down.

We, of course, should have just all stayed down and voted, particularly when we had such a go at Labour for not turning up for one of their own bedroom tax votes but I (totally misguidedly) just did not believe that they would have all their MP resource at the House of Commons for a Private Members' Bill which didn't even propose the abolition of the bedroom tax. Labour are positively gleeful, for them it's payback time, and boy, are they going for it.

Just when I think it's dying down I get word about the press response. The front page of the *Daily Mail* is the headline 'bedroom tax hypocrites' with a special extra feature exclusively for me. The *Daily Express* follow suit with an equally unflattering headline. Terrible day, but one that will be quickly forgotten in the fast-moving indyref. It is a mistake, though, we will not make again.

Saturday 6 September

One of the most ridiculous scare stories pedalled by the No campaign is that there would be a need for a physical border between an independent Scotland and the rest of the UK with the possibility of border guards. It is almost absurd to think that could ever come to pass but yet it is consistently pedalled. Today, for some reason, Ed Miliband revisits the theme today saying 'If you don't want borders vote to stay in the United Kingdom.' Asked if this would include border checks he said 'it would have to be looked at' going on to say 'The last time I looked there were two sides to the border – and we would be in charge of one of them. It would be up to us, not Mr Salmond, to secure our northern border.' Dubbed 'A new Hadrian's wall for Scotland', Miliband now raises the extraordinary prospect of drivers having to stop at manned barriers on the borders to show their passports. This is a theme that plays badly to Labour voters who still have a sense of innate internationalism. Later in the day we get the now obligatory 'clarifications' with a number of Labour figures distancing themselves from these remarks.

It's been the NATO summit in Wales this weekend and we expected a whole load of 'you willnae get in' stories but it's all been rather quiet but almost predictably the Scotsman splashes on its front page this morning a story that says that we, of course, won't get in because 'alliance officials say SNP plans fall short on defence spending'. The paper reports that Scotland would not be allowed into the organisation unless defence spending plans are increased by £500 million over and above First Minister Alex Salmond's current proposals.

But that's about it for NATO coverage. We were braced for more but

I suppose with all the international tensions, Scotland, still lands below most of them.

Sunday 7 September

It has only gone and happened...

This morning we have the first credible opinion poll showing Yes ahead. This is a massive moment and something we have all been hoping for if not praying to the indyref gods for.

It's a small lead but a massive statement. If the referendum was to be held today Yes would win. All over Scotland people involved in either campaign will be reading and rereading this dramatic twist in the indyref saga. The poll is for YouGov and was commissioned by the *Sunday Times* but most papers have it this morning. When the don't knows are stripped out Yes leads No by 51% to 49%.

Where everybody is excited and celebrating the message is to keep focused and keep our feet firmly on the ground. 'Whatever the detail of poll, it is just that – a poll,' tweeted Nicola Sturgeon. 'It's the vote on 18/9 that counts so let's redouble our efforts and stay focused.' I heard late last night that this was on its way and I could hardly believe it. This morning I still don't know how we have got here.

Since the last debate we've noted a change in the campaign, a growing intensity in the Yes vote, a new confidence and fortifying of those who support independence. The Yes case is beginning to spread like wildfire amongst communities everywhere in Scotland through conversations, with whole new cadres of Yes enthusiasts amongst the ordinary, predominately, working people of Scotland emerging. This has gone largely undetected by the media but we've seen it building bit by bit to the point where it is spilling out and overflowing. This is a campaign that now belongs to the communities and people of Scotland and it has assumed a personality of its own.

All of a sudden, it feels like the metropolitan press and commentators have started to catch up with what's going on and there is a lot of talk of the union being on a 'knife edge' and it simply being 'too close to call'. In all the excitement another opinion poll goes barely unnoticed, it's from Panelbase, and almost ironically commissioned by Yes, and it shows us behind by four percentage points. However, even here there is more comforting news, it shows the female vote, where 'Yes' had lagged behind, once undecideds are stripped out, the female–male vote is almost equal at 47% and 48% respectively. The one main group that we have to convince are now becoming convinced of our case.

The response from the Nos is almost immediate. The Chancellor, George Osborne, is on the Marr show promising even more new powers, he even warbles something about a 'devo-max' offer. This is quite extraordinary and has never been mentioned before. Then we have the Scottish Secretary in another broadcast interview talking more of a 'timetable' rather than 'more powers' itself. Later in the afternoon it appears that this 'more powers/devo-max' offer is going to be articulated by Gordon Brown.

'Devo-max' is all they have left. If they have sat round the table and hashed out a real devo-max offer which includes all powers other than defence, foreign affairs and multilateral relations it might just make a difference but I doubt very much this is what they are suggesting at all. The scale of their panic is also demonstrated by the fact that so many of our fellow countrymen have already voted by post. It has therefore been quite an extraordinary day and you can almost sense the UK establishment limbering up to get fully involved in the debate. It's going to be some week.

Before we sign out on what has been an extraordinary day there is a concern that this poll might just have come too early. The Nos will now be energised knowing the scale of the task that now confronts them. There might also be a bit of complacency on our side with many believing that it is won. What we really need now is momentum. Another poll showing us ahead again then another showing us even further ahead. We are now on the cusp of winning and the end of this campaign will be unlike anything we have witnessed in Scottish political life.

Monday 8 September

Left early to get down to Westminster today and it is spooked. Westminster MPS took for granted the repeated reassurance from the complacent group of Scottish Labour MPS. The House of Commons thought that because there are only six SNP MPS out of the 59 MPS from Scotland that this was some sort of true reflection of the public mood. Very few took a real interest in the referendum with most showing signs of irritation or even boredom on the few occasions it has been raised in the Commons.

They complacency meant they have failed to understand and appreciate what the debate has been about and they have responded as a singular Westminster 'establishment' which only went to alienate the Scottish people further.

Today the British House of Commons is effectively paralysed. We have some fun asking points of order about these 'more powers' and if there will be a statement which only adds to the House's unease. My phone doesn't stop ringing with metropolitan journalists wanting a quiet word and a briefing about what's going on. If London thought they were going to have a quiet indyref they have had the illusion shattered now.

In the evening we find out what these 'new powers' are as articulated by Gordon Brown. Instead of using this opportunity to redefine their offer we have nothing other than a timetable with absolutely no 'new powers' on offer at all. Delivered by Gordon Brown from a miner's club in Midlothian it is a timetable that promises either a commitment or a bill to be delivered by Burns Night. In what is a fantastic speech delivered with a compelling passion rarely seen from the former Chancellor he hypes up this barren case as almost some sort of promised land.

The Nos still have a window to try and get on the front foot on this and I'm beginning to hear of all sorts of things about the Nos going much further in defining what a No vote will mean.

Tuesday 9 September

Such is the absolute blind panic that has now descended on Westminster that we hear that all the UK leaders will forsake Prime Minister's Questions and journey up to Scotland instead to embark on a day of campaigning. I raise a point of order in the House asking the Speaker when he was notified of this change. He told me 'in the last two hours' nailing the lie that this was always 'planned'. Westminster is in real peril of falling apart in panic and they are really going to have to steady their nerves. I'm not sure that dispatching the UK establishment to Scotland will do the trick for them though it will certainly lead to a lot more press attention for the No side. Going to be fascinating tomorrow.

After all their predictions of doom and gloom some of that gloom has actually descended on the markets today. Sterling has suffered its biggest fall in a year apparently because of the news that Yes is ahead in the polls. This is also being blamed for a big sell-off of shares in Scottish banking companies such as Bank of Scotland, Standard Life and Lloyds Banking Group. Standard Life has seen its shares fall by 4%, whilst shares in Lloyds and Royal Bank of Scotland fell 3%. Deutsche Bank go further and are saying that: 'The implications of a Yes vote would be huge, and are magnified by the sense of institutional unpreparedness.'

The thing is that the markets all get jittery before any general election and a referendum of this significance is no different. But our friends in the No campaign are ratcheting this up as fears of a precursor of an independent Scotland. Most of this is probably due to concerns over currency and our friends in the Treasury will not do what could possibly squash this in one act – agree to a currency union and bring certainty to the markets. They are probably relieved about all this uncertainty and they are 'certainly' milking it for all its worth. Finally on the financial issues Mark Carney has said that a currency union between the rest of the UK and an independent Scotland would be 'incompatible with sovereignty'. Clearly having been sat on Mark Carney looks like he has finally given into the irresistible pressure of the UK Government to be 'more helpful'. This is what we are now up against.

Wednesday 10 September

With Cameron and Clegg in Scotland, Prime Minister's Questions is left to William Hague and I am down to ask a question. Knowing that the day's session will be almost exclusively on the indyref the Speaker has agreed to take me so at least there will be one question that isn't supporting the No case. In an attempt to wrong-foot Hague, I resist an attack question and instead simply ask him to join me in congratulating the Scottish people in the fantastic way they have conducted the debate. After thinking about it he grudgingly agreed before indulging in the usual 'can't do, won't get' stuff. It worked well with my consensual question contrasting with his hostile tone.

After that it was one interview after another. Sitting in London studios the looks of exasperation on the faces of my English-based colleagues is overwhelming. They even sound like they know it's all up. It's not of course, and there is still a long way to go in this campaign. But this is a seminal point when the UK finally realises that there is now an existential threat to their union and they don't know how to respond.

Meanwhile, it's wall-to-wall coverage of 'the Westminster establishment' trawling round Scotland. This is actually playing out quite well for us and the use of 'Westminster elite' and 'establishment' is circulating everywhere online and gaining currency. It comes across as a very panicky response and these 'leaders' just give an impression of Westminster remoteness. They of course won't share a platform which means they are broken up all over Scotland confusing the media who are having to choose who to cover. They are also saying different things appealing to different constituencies meaning no consistency of message. It's Cameron who receives the lion's share of coverage and for him it's coming down to the 'scale of the decision that the Scottish people will be taking in eight days' time. Sometimes, because it is an election, people can think it is like a general election'. Incredibly he tries to use Scotland's rejection of the Tories as a tactic revealingly saying 'if you are fed-up with the effing Tories, give them a kick and then maybe we will think again. This is a totally different decision to a general election. This is a decision about not the next five years. It is a decision about the next century.' It's almost like for the first time they are recognising that this is about governance.

Ed Miliband is in North Lanarkshire and is saying 'It has been said that the emotional argument lies with independence. Not for me. Not for so many people across our country. Because our hearts lie with you.' Desperately trying to stem the tide of Labour voters signing up with Yes with all sorts of stuff about social justice his trip seems a tribute to working-class Scotland, pits, shipyards and all. Lastly, apparently Nick Clegg's in Selkirk, but I don't think all that many people are bothered either way.

Thursday 11 September

After all this time we are only a week away from the referendum and Scotland has almost descended into a carnival of politics. You can feel it in every community, it exists in every conversation and it is everywhere in this incredible nation of ours. This is an amazing time in Scotland and you can feel history being shaped and played out. This morning about 100 English Labour MPs arrived by train in the most dramatic fashion to save the union. Such is the great humour and incredible atmosphere, particularly in Glasgow, they were met by a man in a rickshaw and loudspeaker who was playing the 'Imperial March' from Star Wars shouting at a bemused group of Labour MPs and the Glasgow public – 'people of Glasgow, bow down to your imperial masters, who have come from England to save the union'. Recognising several of my Labour colleagues they just did not know what hit them. Welcome to Scotland, friends, it's a bit like that just now.

Almost disastrously they then trooped up to the statue of Donald Dewar in Buchanan Street and as a group lined up behind it, leaving them in a stand-off with a group of Yes supporters who 'just happened' to be there. In the middle were all of the UK's press and it descended into who could shout Yes or No loudest. Ed Miliband in attempting to speak to his troops just had a look of 'what the ****', before giving up. The journalist Michael Deacon perhaps summed it up perfectly when he said the scenes were 'ragingly hysterical' and 'borderline psychotic'. Indeed.

As well as coming to 'love' us they also have to wield the stick and today corporate UK is doing their bit for the union. Lloyds Banking Group announce that it will relocate its headquarters from Edinburgh to London. The Royal Bank of Scotland will apparently follow suit, moving its headquarters from Gogarburn in Edinburgh in the event of Scottish independence. Throughout the day RBS clarifies its position in that no jobs will be threatened and it is just about where the plaque is going to be stationed. The Nos are absolutely delighted with this bit of bad news with Danny Alexander saying, 'This is the day the economic case for separation died and reality that independence will cost jobs, investment and growth dawned.' How this will actually play out in a campaign that has become as much about taking on the 'establishment' is uncertain though. In the last few days anti-politics and a desire to almost rewrite how we conduct public life has started to enter the debate and all obviously on the No side. These announcements might only feed that.

Meanwhile over in Edinburgh Alex is hosting a press conference, notionally for the foreign press but with so much going on it inevitably becomes a press crucible. In an extraordinary exchange with the BBC's Nick Robinson which quickly became an all-out assault from the BBC veteran things started to get very heated. First there were shouts of 'bias' as the First Minister responded to a question about the consequences of the banks and businesses deserting Scotland.

Asking why men 'responsible for billions of pounds of profits' should be ignored over the views of the First Minister Alex insisted RBS was just looking to move its 'brass plate' and that any change of HQ would not have any impact on jobs or taxes. Then in a cute move the FM turned the tables on Robinson by brandishing a printout of a BBC website report that quoted Treasury sources revealing that RBS could move. Branding this a leak of 'market sensitive information' which broke basic Treasury rules he said 'I know that the BBC will want to cooperate with the inevitable investigation by the Cabinet Secretary.'

In the news later Robinson reported that the FM didn't answer his question when the FM spent seven minutes giving a more than fulsome response. The BBC are now on the cusp of losing total trust in the referendum and there is real concern about the way that the metropolitan press has descended on Scotland and how they are covering the campaign. We know that none of these people are well disposed to Scottish independence and this is becoming very apparent in the way the referendum is being covered.

Tonight is the last of the 'big' debates in the independence referendum and it is compelling viewing. Coming from the cavernous Hydro it is packed to the gunnels with 16- and 17-year-olds. Nicola Sturgeon and Patrick Harvie represent Yes whilst Ruth Davidson and George Galloway were there for the Nos. For some reason Labour gave up its seat for the unpredictable Galloway and here he is sitting there looking like a very strange man in a hat. Challenged about his comments on rape from Patrick Harvie he almost lost it, then at the end he seemed to compare the SNP with nazis. Repeatedly booed by the audience it was a presentational disaster for the Nos that could only have moved many of them toward yes. Incredible day in the indyref campaign and there are still six to go.

Friday 12 September

The pollster that gave us our first ever lead now has another opinion poll which shows the Nos ahead again. The YouGov poll this morning has No on 52% with Yes on 48%. *The Sun*, which has this poll, says No retook the lead amid fears, particularly among women, that a Yes vote would make the country poorer. The *Times* says – Support for independence Scotland on the slide – says the Yes campaign is 'stalling'. This follows another opinion poll carried out by Survation, it puts the no campaign six points ahead with Yes apparently 'stalling' on 47%, with No on 53%. Did suspect that there was always going to be a bit of a bounce back after a poll showing us ahead as potential No supporters actually see the prospect of actually being defeated but we haven't fallen back by too far and we are still in there. Being slightly behind in the polls also allows us to continue to claim that we are the underdog in this fight. Will be many polls yet and they will all have a story to tell.

In the last few days following the contraction of the polls the Nos have tried to be a bit more detailed, personal and nuanced in their scare stories and heightening concerns. So this week it has been interest rates, borrowing and a focus on household incomes and costs. Today that has been significantly ratcheted up with a raft of supermarkets and retailers warning the Scots of higher prices in the event of independence. So this morning we learn that 'Shoppers will pay for a split, John Lewis and Asda warn.' This is more fertile territory for the Nos and could have an impact. It is all orchestrated of course as we have learned that most of the supermarket bosses were invited to Downing Street earlier in the week. Now, it is possible that Cameron just wanted a chi-chat about supermarket trends but my suspicious nature concludes it was to ensure that they said something 'helpful' in the indyref.

We even learned that there was a cheerleader for the UK Government in the guise of Sir Ian Cheshire, the chief executive of Kingfisher. He enlisted Marc Bolland of Marks and Spencer, and Charlie Mayfield of John Lewis. Cheshire in fact tells us that 'Business leaders need to speak out and get the facts in front of Scottish voters. It's not scaremongering... there are costs and consequences of separation and I think the current system works better.' Well, yes, he would, wouldn't he.

Mad day in Perth as the First Minister and Deputy First Minister conclude their helicopter tour of Scotland's cities in the fair city.

We were originally told that this would be at 4pm but it is almost 5.30pm before Nicola appears. Amazingly hundreds of our supporters hang around to wait for them, as do our friends in the Nos, well aware that they are on their way. I pick up Nicola away from the crowds and walk her down Perth High Street but all of a sudden a mad crowd develops including TV cameras. In a chaotic scrum I lose Nicola and get jostled by No supporters trying to crash our photos and disrupt proceedings.

The Nos have been particularly pious about 'intimidation' and 'threats' but almost gleefully give it out when they get the chance. Perth is unused to such scenes and I hope that the last few days are spared these uncomfortable moments.

I can't stay for Alex as I'm doing my last Yes meeting in my old hometown in Dunfermline. Even when it is all almost all over there is still a huge crowd. Enjoyed talking about my upbringing in Fife and how the values of the area shaped my politics. Will miss these meetings and have really enjoyed taking part in them.

Saturday 13 September

The last Saturday of the campaign and you can almost feel and touch the excitement in the air in the city centre. Both campaigns are here and there is something approaching a carnival atmosphere with practically everyone wearing either a Yes badge or one of their 'No Thanks' stickers. I've organised one last big event in the city centre round the Perthshire singer Dougie MacLean and his iconic song Caledonia. We put the word around last night on social media and there is already an expectant crowd of a few hundred gathered in Perth High Street.

The idea was that one of the regular buskers who is performing in the city centre starts to perform Caledonia and is then joined by our own independence choir, who are then joined by about 15 musicians before Dougie himself appears to pick up the song.

It doesn't quite work out like that. The High Street is too busy for the musicians to get any sort of platform and our busker forgets some of the words! But then Dougie turns up and it is absolutely electric. Silence seems to descend on the High Street and looking round several people are actually close to tears. When Dougie is finished I make a small speech and some Better Together idiot makes a lunge at Dougie and I, but is quickly calmed down by our supporters. It was a fantastic event and everybody is really happy. As we finish we start to see some pictures of elsewhere in Scotland. In Glasgow thousands of Yes supporters have taken to the streets and George Square and Buchanan Street are stowed out. There have never been scenes like this in Scotland and no-one is going to forget this day.

Meanwhile the No campaign had to endure the Orange Order who are having a British 'unity' parade in Edinburgh. Almost ironically this is perhaps the biggest rally the No campaign have managed throughout the whole referendum. This is immensely embarrassing for the Nos who have ran a mile from any association with this divisive group. The images are bad. All over Scotland Yes campaigners are joyfully celebrating this carnival of politics whilst in Edinburgh this group wanders round the capital with their Union Jacks and messages of division. All of the Yes campaign ignore this march and the fear of any flashpoint dissipates. Exhausted we retire to the Greyfriars pub in Perth with Dougie and some of the musicians where more songs are performed. The campaign is coming to a climax now and it almost feels a privilege to be living through such times.

Just before going to bed I hear that the Perth hostage, David Haines, has been executed by the IS jihadists in Iraq. We had all been hoping that he might still get out alive and I have been dealing with the family offering any assistance that they may need. Dreadful stuff and will be huge in the press tomorrow.

Sunday 14 September

I get my first phone call and bid to appear on the media at 6.15am and from then my phone did not stop. Did Radio's 4 and 5 before

7am and Sky had dispatched a van for an 9am interview. This goes on all day and it was actually quite distressing having to give comment on a man who was so brutally murdered. Try to give the view from Perth and how the whole community would be here for the family. Inevitably some of the interviews verge on to the indyref particularly from the many foreign news outlets who have descended on Perth. What is impressive is that so many foreign broadcasters understand all the issues concerning the indyref and they approach these issues without any particular agendas and with a real sensitivity to a city that is in grief following the brutal murder of one of its sons.

The big news today is of course the last of the opinion polls. There are two this morning showing a small swing back to No. A Survation and Opinium poll both give No 53% to Yes 47% but a smaller ICM poll actually gives a 54% to 46% lead. It is absolutely too close to call. After two and a half years the polls are now on a knife edge where last year there was something like a 20% No lead. This is now getting overwhelmingly exciting and people are actually having trouble sleeping trying to figure things out. It is incredible that we go into the last week with the referendum so finely balanced and with a few days still to go there is a sense that there are still a few twists to play out yet.

In the evening I venture down to the concert for Yes in the Usher Hall. Scottish musicians have come together for this last big concert and there is a stellar line up including Mogwai, Amy MacDonald, Franz Ferdinand and Frightened Rabbit. It is a fantastic joyous occasion high on emotion and passion. Get a chance to see some of my colleagues for the last time before the referendum. Everybody is obviously excited and high on adrenalin with a real determination to deliver this. Support from Scottish artists has been incredible and they have helped build support amongst young Scots. Some have emerged as key communicators like Mogwai's Stuart Braithwaite, who has helped ensure that Yes is the overwhelmingly 'cool' option. Leave exhilarated and now totally set for what will be the biggest week in my political life.

Monday 15 September

David Cameron is making his last visit to Scotland today and he is in a very emotional mood. Voice almost quivering, recognising the Tories' unpopularity in Scotland he said 'if you don't like me, I won't be here forever' adding 'I speak for millions of people across England, Wales and Northern Ireland – and many in Scotland, too, who would be utterly heartbroken by the break-up of the United Kingdom. Utterly heartbroken to wake up on Friday morning to the end of the country we love.' As I've said before Cameron makes a very passionate case for the union but he could not be usefully deployed because of the Tory 'problem'. I actually believe that if he had debated with the First Minister he might just have pulled it off. He has therefore had a curious campaign. Here, but not here, engaged, but kept in the background. He is now going back to 10 Downing Street and the next we will hear from him will be after it's all over.

Someone who is not going anywhere is the now ubiquitous Gordon Brown who has become the de-facto leader of the No campaign. Such is his leadership role that he (as an opposition backbencher) is practically making policy on behalf of the Tory Government. In yet another speech he is now saying that a No vote is a vote for change saying 'People want change... after a lengthy and often acrimonious debate, I sense that people want change that can unite Scotland, rather than divide Scotland.' Brown has grown into this role and is much more credible and believable than Alistair Darling. He has been mobilised to stem the tide of Labour voters going to Yes and he has made a gargantuan contribution. This is necessary as all the talk is of the sheer numbers of Labour voters intending to vote Yes. The arrival of the massed ranks of the Labour Party has done nothing to stem the tide of Labour voters coming over to No.

In London there is a unity rally in Trafalgar Square. Looking at the pictures there looks like that there might be up to a thousand people amongst the lions and the fountains. Organised by the Tory-supporting Spectator magazine it looks a particularly depressing affair. Bob Geldof makes a speech unaware of the irony of an Irishman requesting that we Scots remain 'British'. There are also contributions from Dan Snow, the main figure behind the 'love bombing' letter and other people I don't recognise. This rather pathetic affair has to be compared and contrasted with the unity rally at the end of the Quebec referendum when a million people from the rest of Canada went to Quebec asking them to stay. Almost to compound the failure of the 'love bombing' campaign and how they have managed to get it almost entirely wrong, David Beckham has entered stage left calling on Scotland to remain in the Union and preserve the 'historic bond' which is 'the envy of the entire world'. The 'love bombing' is now over but it has been a campaign that has singularly failed to detonate.

Tuesday 16 September

Today will go down in indyref history as the day of 'the vow'.

The front page of the *Daily Record* reveals the last big move in the independence referendum and it is a huge intervention. In what could only be described as a 'historic' joint statement it is signed by Prime Minister David Cameron, Deputy Prime Minister Nick Clegg and Labour leader Ed Miliband it outlines powers to be devolved to Holyrood in the event of a 'No' vote. The 'vow' includes new powers for the Scottish Parliament, that the parliament will be enshrined as an 'irreversible part of the British constitution', the continuation of the Barnett allocation, and a 'guarantee of fairness to Scotland'. This statement was apparently brokered by former Prime Minister Gordon Brown. It is simply an incredible document and it will have a massive impact on the last couple of days in the campaign.

Part of it reads 'Because of the continuation of the Barnett allocation for resources, and the powers of the Scottish Parliament to raise revenue, we can state categorically that the final say on how much is spent on the NHS will be a matter for the Scottish Parliament.'

There can be no doubt about the impact this will have and being introduced at such a late hour, this could determine the result of the referendum. The whole referendum campaign has been about owning the 'change' agenda. We of course had the biggest claim to this as we genuinely want to change Scotland from its current status as part of the UK. Thought the last couple of years the Nos have wrestled with this issue and have haphazardly tried to concoct some sort of joint change/more powers agenda. Today they have got it together with almost perfect timing hitting all the right chords.

Phone round a few colleagues to get the response and there is genuine concern that it could kill us. I go into my local newsagents to secure a physical copy and there are only a couple of copies of the *Daily Record* left, apparently in the words of the always affable man behind the counter in the Craigie co-op 'it has been shifting like hot cakes'. This is really bad and we have no moves left.

Trying to get the Vow out of my head I strap on the loudspeaker to a van be-decked in Yes regalia and take to the streets of Perth. This is now the time to try and get a bit of excitement on the streets and I love being out and about delivering the message. In the city centre we still have our stall out and there are groups working in each of the towns and villages in Perthshire. We've even started to give out 'reading' cards. Cards which we ask our support to hand to the Yes representative at the polling station on Thursday. Everywhere there is activity and this is happening everywhere in Scotland.

One man not feeling the love is Ed Miliband who was forced to abandon a campaign walkabout yesterday after clashes between yes and no campaigners in the St James Centre in Edinburgh. This allowed him to use the now familiar 'ugly side' of the referendum campaign saying debates should be conducted in a civilised way. This, though, is street campaigning, and when you take to the streets you invite a response. Labour used to understand these things. No-one now listening to this stuff anymore and a real shame that Labour still talking down what is in fact a great spectacle of politics. We're all too busy enjoying the closing moments of this wonderful campaign to really take much notice of their whinging now.

Wednesday 17 September

After some two and a half years we are at the last day of the independence campaign. All of us are increasingly exhausted but excited beyond anything ever experienced in Scotland's political life. It has been a huge journey with so many ups and downs, false dawns and impossible turns. All the talk is of a massive turnout. Eighty per cent plus is being touted and that might just be secured. Everyone is engaged and the feeling on the streets is just electric. Out and about today I realise that this is the last time I will be doing this and I will miss it so much. As a politician you never get the opportunity to secure a lifetime ambition and tomorrow I just might get the chance to realise my life work of an independent Scotland.

I spend the morning in the rural areas of my constituency touring in the Yes van, stopping to speak to people in the high streets of the various villages and towns in my massive constituency. In Pitlochry I meet a 16-year-old girl who is beyond excited about being given the right to vote. She said she researched all the issues before making her choice and is just so grateful that she is getting this opportunity. I didn't even bother asking her which way she was voting.

This contest has gone right down to the wire and all within margins of error, making it even more of a thrilling contest. Hopefully our support is more motivated and sensing that it is within our grasp will ensure they get out and get us over the line. Hearing from colleagues that our own private polling is showing us leading 54% to 46%.

Do I think we can do it? I think we can but fear we won't. The only thing that makes me doubtful about the final outcome is how the newly registered voters will go and just how many of the 'anti-politics' vote will actually come out and support us. The Yes campaign is now a behemoth of independence parties, socialists, anti-politics individuals and the disenfranchised looking for substantial political change. An alliance that would have seemed impossible only a few months ago. There are now so many variables out there that all predictions are almost a waste of breath.

Meanwhile the eve of poll pitches are being transmitted. First up is Gordon Brown (who else) who delivers what I have to concede is an absolutely stonking speech. He doesn't say anything new but it is filled with passion and a real love for the union, his idea of Britain and the ties that he believes unite us throughout the UK. Brown has certainly come into his own and if it is a No vote the unionists will owe a great deal of gratitude to this curious, flawed and somewhat strange man, who has found his niche in defending the UK.

Lastly it is the First Minister and his last speech is coming from the Concert Hall in Perth. We are all obviously delighted that he has chosen Perth for the last campaign message. This was only announced last night and the 2,000 tickets available were snapped up in minutes. We organise a great reception for him outside the hall and there are drummers and pipers and hundreds of people who can't get in. Inside there is an introduction from Elaine C Smith before a speech from Nicola Sturgeon. Then the First Minister takes the stage and the cheers go through the roof. After his initial wobble at the first debate Alex has played a blinder and where his longevity now means he is seen as a divisive figure there is no doubt about his box office and down to earth campaigning abilities. He also doesn't say anything that we haven't heard before but he says it all so well. It is all about our opportunity to make history and grasp this moment. Everyone in the hall is high with the excitement of it all and we leave hoping to make history tomorrow.

Thursday 18 September

It's finally here. I joined the SNP to great fanfare in 1995 when we had four MPs and less than 20% in the opinion polls. Now today we are asking the people of Scotland whether they want our nation to be an independent country. It has been an incredible journey and I feel quite emotional as I go and cast my vote in Craigie Church just round the corner from where I stay. The polling station is mobbed and I recognise all the returning officer's staff who said it has been going like a fair since they opened at seven in the morning. I make a tour of the polling stations round the city and they are all the same.

Turnout is going to be huge and people have voted early. In North Muirton in Perth someone approaches me with a series of questions as he still has not made up his mind but so wants to vote... I think I convince him to vote Yes but after all the debate I wonder just how many are like him, still unsure how to cast their vote. Even the No representatives at the polling station just looked on in bemusement that we are still discussing the issues.

In the afternoon I head up to the rural areas of my constituency and if anything they are even busier. Here the Nos seem to be out in real force and it would seem that they have their support mobilised. I go back to the office to help the 'get the vote out effort' at the crucial early evening period to be told that this is probably an unnecessary exercise from Yes Scotland. Everyone apparently is voting and looking at our knock-up sheets most actually have. I therefore do another tour of Perth with the van and the loudspeaker. Call it a night about 9pm and return home for a break and something to eat before the count. Can't relax though, and venture down to the Bell's Sports Centre for the Perth and Kinross count early. Here we go. Can we, can we?

Evening of 18/19 September

An expectant Bell's is mobbed. All the registered groups have the right to have a full complement of representatives and there are people from all the campaigning groups such as Women for Indy and Business for Scotland. All elected representatives have also been invited and there was an invitation extended to the Head and Deputy Head Boys and Girls from all the Perth High Schools. The start of the count is always a curious affair as we await the first boxes to arrive. We are all organised for the ballot box samples and there is lots of nervous pacing of the cavernous sports hall.

The first boxes arrive at about 11.30pm, later than usual. By midnight there is a steady stream of boxes being opened and their contents spilled in front of the many counters and supervising campaigners. Already we are hearing from counts elsewhere that it is not going well. Examining the first boxes it is apparent that we are clearly behind. Surely this can still be turned around?

A sickening knot is developing in the pit of my stomach and I look round at colleagues who are also observing these early votes with the same degree of apprehension. Cast iron discipline prevails and the sampling is conducted in the usual Perthshire military manner. The first declaration is from Clackmannan. A decisive win for No in a county that we really needed to have won if we are to prevail. Still early, though...

As further boxes are opened we look well behind in Perth and Kinross and the No campaign are looking increasingly happy. More declarations, more success for No. But then there is a bit hope. In a series of results from East Dunbartonshire, Dundee and North Lanark, we win, and for one beautiful moment we are slightly ahead. Didn't last long though, as more declarations pushed our percentage share further down and down. This isn't going to happen now and everyone in the Bell's Sport Centre knows it.

Hearing good things from Glasgow. Could a huge Yes vote from there bring us back into the game? We're grabbing at anything now. Perth and Kinross is declared at about 4am and we get beat soundly, 60% to 40%. I head home totally despondent knowing that we are beat. Glasgow is finally declared and we won, but not enough to make a difference, and it is now officially all over.

At 6am the First Minister makes a speech conceding the referendum and congratulating the No campaign. A dignified and composed Alex says we will now hold the unionist parties to their promises of more powers. An hour later the Prime Minister appears from Downing Street accepting the victory. In his speech he seems to say some things about England and more powers for the rest of the UK, there's also some strange stuff about voting rights of Scottish MPs! What on earth is this? It almost seems unnecessarily provocative and an exercise in rubbing our faces in it. The two speeches from First Minister and Prime Minister could not be more different in their tone and intent.

Finally the Chief Returning Officer, Mary Pitcaithly, announced the final result. Yes 44.7%, No 53.3%. It's all over we have lost. I lie down for a break, absolutely exhausted and totally and utterly bereft.

Friday 19 September

Must have dozed off and awoken by the first of several phone calls from journalists wanting my response to the results. Ignore them all. Can't help but look at the extended results programmes on all channels and the scenes from the various counts. There are of course the looks of jubilation on the faces of the victors in the No camp and looks of despair and despondency on the faces of the many friends and colleagues I recognise in the Yes camp. Both camps seem to accept the result in good grace and there is a strange stillness as we try to appreciate the significance of what has just transpired. Try to examine the national picture from across the country and make a few calls to close colleagues to see how they are.

Then there is an announcement that there will be a further statement from the First Minister from Bute House. Expecting this to be a further concession speech Alex instead announces that he is to stand down as First Minister and leader of the SNP. Nothing could further confirm that this is now all over. If anyone could claim to have secured this referendum it is Alex Salmond, and this complex but flawed man has led the campaign from certain defeat to almost victory.

The rest of the day I spend in a strange, numbed state before going out in the evening to meet a few close colleagues in the Yes campaign in Perth. Have to concede that the consumption of alcohol could not be categorised of the 'responsible' category. Everybody is just wondering, what do we do now?

The last few days and weeks have been just about the most traumatic, exhilarating and emotionally draining I have ever known in my political life. Yet, I still feel hopeful and optimistic about the future of my country. I've seen my nation accept the verdict of the Scottish people with good grace and other than some disgraceful scenes from George Square, where a squad of hardline unionists descended upon a peaceful vigil of disappointed Yes supporters, there has not been the rancour predicted by those who don't understand the resilience of this wonderful country. I have seen the incredible spirit of those who have campaigned selflessly to the point of exhaustion in this referendum vow to continue so that the energy and engagement created by the independence referendum continues to have a voice. This is why our country is the most remarkable place and why we will endure, regroup and progress.

Scotland has spoken and rejected independence by a clear majority but yet we don't feel defeated or diminished. Nothing will disabuse me from the belief that the people who live and work in Scotland are those best placed to make the decisions about Scotland's future. Scotland rejected independence but it seems to have also developed a new character and political personality.

Meanwhile the never-ending cycle of democracy goes on as we now turn our attention to the general election in eight short months' time. There's a sense that this referendum has changed Scottish politics for ever and that things simply will not go on as before.

Whatever that is, it's all over for now.

Luath Press Limited

committed to publishing well written books worth reading

LUATH PRESS takes its name from Robert Burns, whose little collie Luath (*Gael.*, swift or nimble) tripped up Jean Armour at a wedding and gave him the chance to speak to the woman who was to be his wife and the abiding love of his life. Burns called one of the 'Twa Dogs' Luath after Cuchullin's hunting dog in Ossian's *Fingal*. Luath Press was established in 1981 in the heart of Burns country, and is now based a few steps up the road from Burns' first lodgings on Edinburgh's Royal Mile. Luath offers you distinctive writing with a hint of unexpected pleasures.

Most bookshops in the UK, the US, Canada, Australia, New Zealand and parts of Europe, either carry our books in stock or can order them for you. To order direct from us, please send a £sterling cheque, postal order, international money order or your credit card details (number, address of cardholder and expiry date) to us at the address below. Please add post and packing as follows: UK – £1.00 per delivery address; overseas surface mail – £2.50 per delivery address; overseas airmail – £3.50 for the first book to each delivery address, plus £1.00 for each additional book by airmail to the same address. If your order is a gift, we will happily enclose your card or message at no extra charge.

Luath Press Limited
543/2 Castlehill
The Royal Mile
Edinburgh EH1 2ND
Scotland
Telephone: 0131 225 4326 (24 hours)
Email: sales@luath.co.uk
Website: www.luath.co.uk